Venı *in* Ireıand

Quest for
the Modern Celtic Soul

Venturing
in Ireland

Quest for
the Modern Celtic Soul

Edited by Barbara J. Euser & Connie Burke

TRAVELERS' TALES
an imprint of Solas House
PALO ALTO

Travelers' Tales and Travelers' Tales Guides are trademarks of Travelers' Tales, an imprint of Solas House, 853 Alma Street, Palo Alto, California 94301.

For permission to print essays in this volume, grateful acknowledgement is made to the holders of copyright named on pages 242-249.

For more information on visiting Ireland, contact Tourism Ireland at www.discoverireland.com or call 1-800-223-6470.

Front and back cover photographs copyright by Connie Burke.
Front cover: *Fastnet Lighthouse at Mizen Head, the southernmost point in the Republic of Ireland.*
Back cover top: *Sailboats moored in Kinsale harbor.*
Back cover bottom: *Houses along the waterfront in Kinsale, County Cork, Ireland.*

Cover and interior design by Sabine Reifig, Menta Design, Athens, Greece, www.menta.gr, using fonts Scurlock (for initial letters) and Sabon.

CATALOGUING DATA
Venturing in Ireland: Quest for the Modern Celtic Soul/edited by Barbara J. Euser and Connie Burke.

ISBN-10: 193236156-1
ISBN-13: 978-193236156-8

1. Ireland—Description and travel. 2. Ireland—Social life and customs. 3. County Cork—Description and travel. 4. County Cork—Social life and customs. I. Title. II. Euser, Barbara J. III. Burke, Connie.

First Edition
Printed in the United States of America
10 9 8 7 6 5 4 3 2 1

To the mothers of emigrants from Ireland.

To my father Anthony Euser and
his mother Barbara Van Namen Euser.
Anthony left the Netherlands in 1947 and
never saw his mother again.

To my mother, the late Chrysanthy "Soula" Leones
and her mother Kanelia Mazaraki Kataga.
Chrysanthy left Greece in 1947
and never saw her mother again.

CONTENTS

Contents

PREFACE

enturing in Ireland: Quest for the Modern Celtic Soul is the product of a writers' workshop held in County Cork, Ireland during the summer of 2007. Our group consisted of a dozen writers, instructors and contributing editors Linda Watanabe McFerrin and Joanna Biggar, and workshop organizers Connie Burke and myself. We were all inspired by the people we met and the places we visited in this complex and enchanting isle. As Linda McFerrin said, the anthology reads almost like a novel, as people, places and experiences intertwine from one essay to the next.

For ten days we stayed at the Bellevue Bed and Breakfast in Myrtleville, owned and operated by Benny and Gaby Neff. They sent us out in the morning fortified with exceptionally full Irish breakfasts and welcomed us home at night, sometimes with dinner, other times with spiritual sustenance of music and song.

We were assisted in our quest by a number of people and organizations whom I would like to thank: Ambassador Margaret Hennessey; Lorraine O'Brien; and the Irish Tourism Board that provided support, including our visits to Charles Fort and Desmond Castle, Kinsale; Mizen Head Visitor Centre; Lismore Castle Estate; Lismore Heritage Centre; Cobh Heritage Museum (The Queenstown Project); Crosshaven House; Cork City Gaol and Cork City Museum.

Irish writers in particular captured our attention. We met with poet Desmond O'Grady, whom Nobel prize winner

Seamus Heaney called "one of the senior figures in Irish literary life, exemplary in the way he committed himself over the decades to the vocation of poetry." Alice Taylor, celebrated memoirist, welcomed us into her home. Writers known and unknown from the Cork City Gaol chilled and inspired us with their haunting texts. The anonymous author of the ninth century poem about a writer and his cat made us smile.

Music surrounded us in Ireland and features in a number of the essays. I was particularly impressed with the accessibility of music: in pubs we visited, everyone seemed to participate and we were welcomed to add our voices to the chorus.

In addition to today's inhabitants of Ireland, we encountered the legacy of Irish emigrants. The tradition of the American Wake, held for emigrants who might never return home, resonated with me. My father left his native Netherlands at the age of twenty-four, younger than my elder daughter is today, to emigrate to the United States. He was the oldest of six brothers. He might have eventually taken over the family farm, but he sought greater opportunities. When he left, his mother cried, fearing she would never see him again. She never did. She suffered a fatal stroke two years after his departure.

It is the intricately woven tapestry of emotion and practicality, magic and mysticism, heartache and song that defines Ireland. I hope these pages will draw you into the richness of Ireland as you join us in our quest for the modern Celtic soul.

—BARBARA J. EUSER

FOREWORD

Ireland, land of soft rain, green grass, poets, writers, strong drink, and even stronger women. Enough of the clichés, Ireland and the Irish have been stereotyped to death, ever since the first talking pictures when American actors thought they could speak with an Irish accent.

However in June this year at least one cliché was true, an invasion of strong women from all over the world stormed Cork, oh and they were writers and poets, so maybe the clichés work. The Writer's Workshop brought all the women [and one man] whose stories appear in this book together. To eat, drink, play and work, and in the spaces between be soothed by the soft accents, baffled by Irish humour and encouraged to drink the black brew, Guinness (sure it's good for what ails ye).

The stories recount each writer's own special response to this special island, to each other, their lives and loves far away and the delicious feeling of liberty and fellowship which comes from being able to take time out of the everyday and enter into a magical realm, where friendship is celebrated through exploration, discovery and the creation of stories.

Stories tell us a lot, about ourselves, about a place, and of course about the writer, and these writers have wonderful stories to tell. I am proud they chose my homeland for their unique gathering and even prouder that the resulting book demonstrates the power of place in inspiring imaginations and nurturing creative souls.

—MAUREEN WHEELER *Lonely Planet Publications*

ILLUSTRATIONS

Ireland
circa 700 A.D.

MAIN KINGDOMS

NORTHERN
UI NEILL

ULAID

AIRGIALLA

CONNACT

SOUTHERN
UI NEILL
• Newgrange
BrúNa Bóinne
• Tara
◉ Dublin

LAIGIN

MUNSTER

• Drombeg Stone Circle

Ireland
today

COUNTIES

DONEGAL

NORTHERN IRELAND

Belfast

LEITRIM

SLIGO

MONAGHAN

MAYO

ROSCOMMON

CAVAN

LONGFORD

LOUTH

MEATH

IRISH SEA

GALWAY

WESTMEATH

DUBLIN

IRELAND

Dublin

OFFALY

Tullamore

KILDARE

R. Liffey

ATLANTIC OCEAN

CLARE

LAOIS

WICKLOW

TIPPERARY

CARLOW

KILKENNY

Limerick

LIMERICK

Tipperary

WEXFORD

Killarney

R. Blackwater

Waterford

WATERFORD

KERRY

R. Lee

Cork

CORK

CELTIC SEA

Mizen Head

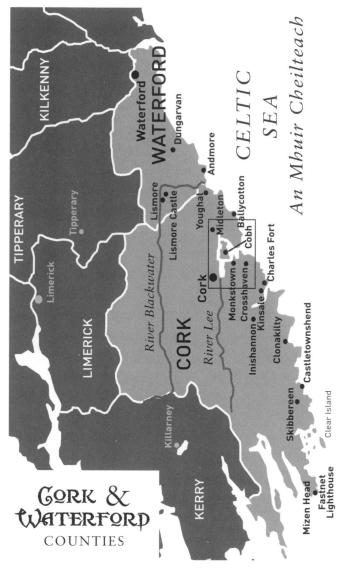

CORK &
WATERFORD
COUNTIES

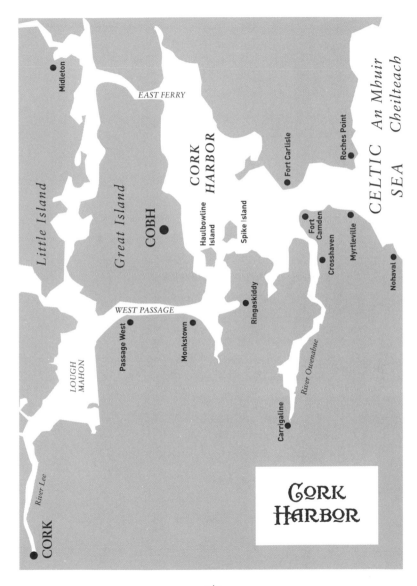

The Irish Tongue

❀

Munster Irish is a rich tongue
with a foreign tone from foreign aid;
a clear sound, clear as song,
crisp, clever, finely grained.

Though Hebrew they claim is the oldest
and Latin and Greek the most learned,
on none of them have we trespassed
for phrase or sentence no matter how worded.

—DESMOND O'GRADY

IRISH COMFORT FOOD

LENNY KARPMAN

In my family, comfort food is survival nostalgia from Czarist Russia and its pogroms, pathos from past struggles on New York's Lower East Side during the Depression, and the safe harbor of family and good friends—all on a single plate. It is the appetizer belly-filler of lean and hungry days, the entrée of improved times without fear, and, finally, the dessert of emancipation, memory, and love that fuels the creation of a legacy for the children.

Ireland's County Cork has a history that parallels that of my clan, escape from chronic fear, and a cuisine evolved from minimal sustenance to sophisticated splendor. For centuries, all Irish food was considered comfort food. There was no cuisine beyond simple, traditional, home-style belly-fillers. Some called it dull. Then came the culinary revolution. Have the traditional edible pacifiers moved aside or do they still reign supreme?

I'm in tiny Myrtleville, overlooking the Celtic Sea in south-central County Cork, searching for a sign or prophet to direct me. Here I meet Gaby Neff, the guide and guru to my quest. She is hostess and chef to our group of seekers of Irish essence and writers of odes and tales of travel. We hale from North America, Europe, and Central America. Gaby is proud grandmother of six, but hardly looks it. Coiffed in short blond hair, she is trim and graceful. Her Swiss accent has overtones of Irish lilt after twelve emerald years. Her husband, Benny Neff, a native Corkonian, is our host, guide, and balladeer.

At six forty-five in the morning, Gaby enters the kitchen and lets me perch at her elbow while she creates her distinctive version of Irish brown soda bread for breakfast. So begins my first tutorial on comfort food. *The dry ingredients go into a mixing bowl—one half pound each of stone-ground whole-wheat and white multipurpose flour, a handful of rolled oats, and a teaspoon each of salt and sifted baking soda. She mixes them well, drizzles in a tablespoon of dark molasses, and mixes again. She adds a special Swiss twist, a handful of black walnut pieces. A pint of buttermilk completes the recipe. Chef Gaby adds it one splash at a time, incorporating it evenly with a plastic pastry spatula until the batter is moist, but not sticky. If too dry, she adds more buttermilk, if too moist, a little more flour. Hers is perfect. On a floured cutting board, she caresses it into a flat-topped round and pays homage to the Creator by indenting the surface top to bottom and side to side with a cross. She pops it into a preheated 400 F. oven for forty minutes on a baking sheet and ambrosia fills the air with the beckoning morning scent.*

Gaby lifts the loaf out of the oven and cools it on a wire rack in the backyard, covered, to keep the air squadron of crows away. Other soda bread makers vary the proportions of flour from all white to all brown. They use sugar, honey or molasses, seldom add oats to the batter and skip the walnuts. Most soda bread makers prepare a similar crossed round. Others shape uncrossed loaves in a deep pan and may use soured milk instead of buttermilk. None does it better than Gaby.

Yeast bread keeps better in an airtight tin than does soda bread. Gaby caramelizes her stale walnut soda bread into a praline facsimile and adds it to homemade ice cream.

Her bread is not just a breakfast treat. It is also a mandatory accompaniment of the king of Irish comfort food, Irish stew.

When they had more than just potatoes, the Irish added mutton, carrots, onions, salt and pepper and "filled their bellies so full within of jolly good ale" and stew. In every tradition worldwide, poor people filled their bellies with starches, added a few vegetables and what little meat, fish or fowl they could muster. My Russian grandmother often fed her family of eight on boiled potatoes and carrots and bits of pickled herring. In France, bits of pork and poultry evolved into *cassoulet*. In Italy, beans, pasta and bits of meat morphed into *minestrone* or *pasta faggioli*. In Spain, rice, shellfish, peas and chicken necks, in a wide shallow pot designed for an open fire in the fields, produced *paella*. *Kasha* (buckwheat groats) and pig parts were a

Ukrainian staple. Cabbage rolls stuffed with chopped pork or beef and wheat filler fed people in Poland. *Couscous* with lamb bits and peppers fit the bill in North Africa and rice bowls topped with lesser amounts of all kinds of protein and cooked vegetables nourished most of Asia.

In more prosperous times, these starvation barriers became nostalgic comfort foods as ingredients improved and portions grew larger. They stirred memories of home, childhood, motherly tenderness, contentment and surcease from stress. In Ireland, tender cuts of lamb replaced the shoe-leather-tough mutton of leaner times and shortened stewing time. Thyme improved flavor. Potatoes were added near the end of the slow cooking process or were prepared separately to keep them from disintegrating into the stew. Quality broth replaced water as the cooking liquid.

A good composite modern recipe for Irish stew is as follows: *Heat a quart of liquid, lamb, beef or chicken broth. To the simmering broth, add three pounds of bite-size pieces of lean lamb, three medium onions peeled and quartered, six medium carrots peeled and cut into half-inch logs, four sprigs of fresh thyme, a tablespoon of coarse salt and a teaspoon of black pepper. Simmer on top of the stove or in the oven for about an hour and a half, until the meat is tender. Thicken with a tablespoon of roux or cornstarch dissolved in water. Serve with a side of hot salted boiled potatoes sprinkled with chopped parsley. Don't forget the brown soda bread.*

To my palate, Gaby's less traditional version of Irish stew is a notch above the others. She thickens with a handful (about two tablespoons) of red lentils added early in the cooking and adds about a teaspoon each of rosemary from the garden and minced garlic. Neither dominates the basic flavor. Both enhance it and make it deliciously complex. A pinch of caraway does the same.

I found other noteworthy variations on my culinary quest. At the Farmgate Café in Cork City, a great place to sample traditional comfort food, they include parsnips aplenty in their Irish stew. At Darina Allen's Balleymaloe, the nation's top cooking school, they use mutton stock, layer ingredients, and top with potatoes late in the stewing to keep them intact. In a pub in Dublin, only blocks away from the brewery that once was the world's largest, they start with half Guiness stout and half chicken stock. In another Dublin location, it's beef, barley and Guiness that hardly tastes like Irish stew at all.

Of the three Irish stouts, Beamish and Murphy's are brewed in Cork. Beamish is the sweetest, Murphy's the lightest and Guiness the most bitter. I like a pint of stout with my stew, but not in it. I feel it adds nothing to the taste.

Does comfort food need to be simple and home-style? Not when you observe the foods that give solace to modern-day Irish movers and shakers. Upscale dining has arrived in County Cork with fresh and varied local ingredients enhanced by world-wide spices, elegant sauces and style akin to California cuisine. It is hardly traditional, but paradoxically comforting to many because it is cleansed of any association with prior hard times. While at the bar in Cork, customers Irene and Rob explained that they found "no comfort at all in food that has the bitter taste of oppression in every bite."

I had the opportunity to sample the upscale, classy cuisines of Jim Edwards in postcard-perfect Kinsale, at Finders Inn Restaurant on a narrow tree-lined country road in Nohaval and at Paradiso in Cork City with its exquisite creative vegetarian offerings. I got to sample superb crab claws in garlic butter, steamed mussels in beurre blanc, scallops in mornay sauce, lobster, monkfish in ginger-lime sauce, crispy roast duckling in orange sauce, pink and juicy rosemary-scented rack of lamb and delicious poached salmon with the taste and texture of the wild variety, at a time of the year when it had to have been farmed. These dishes were all served, however, with the traditional staples of brown soda bread and lots of potatoes.

Some inns and pubs even offer items more familiar to North American comfort food seekers: macaroni and cheese, chicken soup, meatloaf and mashed potatoes, chicken in the pot, bagels and lox, chocolate pudding, chocolate-chip cookies and mugs of hot cocoa.

This represents quite a departure from the times of mutton, pig parts, cabbage and potatoes flavored only with salt and pepper. If I were a dining guide in County Cork, I would steer people to one very nice meal in the cozy, living-room atmosphere of Finders Inn Restaurant, where they could spend a relaxing evening feasting away from the tourist trail. If Kinsale were already part of the itinerary, I'd suggest that they might find comparable food at Jim Edwards, but they should be forewarned. The crowd is made up of boisterous fellow tourists, shepherded in and out for seatings at seven and nine.

I would also recommend a traditional venue such as the restaurant on the balcony above the English Market, Farmgate Café, for a one-time experience of old-time favorites with strange-sounding names such as tripe and drisheen, lamb livers, champ, roasted bacon loin, colcannon and Clonakilty black pudding.

For many, comfort emanates more from music, ale and comradery of the local pub, than the food. Despite the emergence of gastro-pubs with more emphasis on fine edibles than in days past, pub menus may appear Spartan, but, as compensation, servings are large. Stouts and ales are still the drinks of choice.

For more authentic dining experiences, I would wish others the good fortune of finding a B&B like Bellevue in Myrtleville and a chef as talented as Gaby Neff, who can deftly prepare dishes from the old and new compendia and explain the differences. She makes breakfast every day: farm-fresh eggs to specification, Irish bacon, breakfast sausage, Clonakilty black pudding studded with crunchy barley, grilled mushrooms, French toast, vanilla flavored crêpes and, on occasion, locally smoked salmon. The buffet is always laden with fresh fruit, five cereals and two toasted seeds, yogurt and orange juice. On the festively set table are decanters of hot coffee, milk and pots of tea, marmalade and warm brown soda bread. Add a second cup of coffee, sipped leisurely with good friends and that's as comforting as it gets for me.

Roddy's Irish

Doreen Wood

As I peered through the partially drawn lace curtains on that narrow Cork City side street in southern Ireland, I thought of that lovely Doyle refrain, "But she's grand."

He says this about Paula Spencer, the indefatigable heroine in his novel, *Paula Spencer*. Ever since my introduction to Roddy Doyle's work, I have been intrigued by his depictions of the working class Irish. As I scoured the city streets, the shops and department stores of Cork and peeked into lamp-lit living quarters, I wanted to gain some understanding of the indomitable Irish spirit that has persisted through centuries of difficulties, famines, uprisings, "troubles" with the English. What has carried these people through such thick and thin?

Farther north in the city of Dublin, I'd spent a wonderful afternoon at the Dublin Writers' Museum, located in an eighteenth century house at 18 Parnell Square, in the hub of this lively city. Its collections feature first edition books and memorabilia of Irish writers who've made an important contribution to Irish or international literature. I listened and looked carefully as their portraits and busts peered at me from the building's high-ceilinged walls. I saw Jonathan Swift, social satirist, familiar to many for his novel, *Gulliver's Travels*, which portrayed the plight of poor children in seventeenth century Ireland. I saw James Joyce, whose epic, *Ulysses*, unfolds in all the squalor and monotony of early twentieth century Dublin. William Butler Yeats, also well represented in the collection, didn't necessarily write about the poor, but concentrated on the human condition. I was thrilled to be a writer momentarily in their company in this tiny country that has produced four Nobel Laureates in literature: Yeats, Shaw, Beckett and Heaney. Historically, it seems, most Irish people love to talk, love to tell stories—and love language. So do I.

These authors measured the pulse of their times. They railed against class distinctions, injustices, and the ruling power of their church. Today, like his predecessors, contemporary author Roddy Doyle describes working class life as it really is, rough and tough, but also with beauty and tenderness. The Dublin Writers' Museum bookshop shelves a complete collection of Doyle's works. Formerly a teacher in the Kilbarrack area of north Dublin, also the area where he grew up, Doyle writes unsettling novels, based on working class experience in the latter half of the twentieth century. His 1993 tale of the interior life of a ten-year-old boy, *Paddy Clarke Ha Ha Ha*, won the

Booker Prize, Britain's highest literary award. His more recent novels, *The Woman Who Walked into Doors* and *Paula Spencer* focus on the tribulations and grit of heroine Paula Spencer.

Doyle's musical sense of rhythm and gifted dialogue pulled me along in a way that made me want to meet Paula and get to know her.

At first, my imagination ran away with me. I'd taken the train south to join my group of writers in County Cork and was immediately on the prowl. Four days after my arrival, I strolled down bustling Patrick Street, in the main shopping district of Cork City, looking to my left and to my right, hoping to spot Doyle's Paula. Wandering through Debenham's Department store, I saw plenty of youths dressed in the latest Gen-Y garments, and wispy-haired elderly ladies in boxy plaid suits, clutching bulky carry-alls. I listened to the singsong cadence in their incessant chatter. No Paula.

Then, I drew a breath of relief. Ah, there she was, standing in a queue at a bus stop on the wide thoroughfare flanked by three-story buildings. She was as I'd expected: of middling height, her lanky auburn hair brushing the collar of her son's cast-off anorak. Her feet, no doubt, were hurting and her back was beginning to go into spasms. She was, I was sure, aching to be in her own kitchen, dreaming of resting her feet on a chair and pouring from a hot pot of tea. She was on her way home to her row house after a long day of work: a morning job cleaning a big house on Ballinlough Road where they paid her in cash, then a late afternoon job wiping and dusting in an office building in uptown Cork. I imagined she was thinking of her almost empty refrigerator, with just a few spuds in the bottom drawer, and had just stopped in at a grocery shop to pick up some sausages for herself and Jack and Nuala, her two teen-aged children still living at home. As she checked out at the till, I'll bet she mused about how things would get better.

That's what I was looking for in *my* fictional Paula Spencer, probably because Paula's life seemed to mirror the experiences in my own early life. In my home city of Winnipeg, Canada, like Paula, I'd stood at bus stops at ten o'clock at night, with a sore back and aching feet, longing to get home and just sit down. My mother was at home with her ninth new baby. We had very little money. I was still at school and worked as much as I could. One short-lived job, I remember, was at a bowling alley in the days before electronic pinsetters. When careening bowling balls came down the lane felling the pins, my task was to jump in to reset them.

I'd thought, then, "You do what you have to do."

Later, in Cork City, I walked from the city center, across the Southgate Bridge over the River Lee and passed by the impos-ing St. Finbarre's Cathedral, an edifice with much Anglican his-tory. I found myself on Lee Street, struck by the many patterns of crisp lace curtains in the windows of the row houses, and by the brightly painted doors and neatly swept stoops. One tall, narrow window must have been opened for some fresh air because I heard a clock inside chiming the hour. An ironing board stood open in a corner of the interior. I saw a fringed lamp casting light from behind an overstuffed chair, a seated figure holding up a newspaper. On a round table I spotted a teapot with creamer, sugar bowl, and matching teacups sitting beside it. It was a china pattern very familiar to me: translucent Belleek porcelain sprayed with pale green shamrocks.

I already knew these people, even though I had not been to Cork City before, and though the year was 2007. In my mind, I went back to the 1950s, to the Hunniford's, Irish immigrants on Logan Avenue in Winnipeg, Canada. Joan Hunniford was my very best girlfriend, forever earning my devotion by inviting me to her tenth birthday party when no one else would. I wore my one new garment of the year, a black serge school tunic. For years after that I became a fixture at her house, escaping the harsh reality of my very poor family. Their ironing board was always up at Joan's house, white shirts still steaming from a good press. At exactly ten o'clock every evening Mrs. Hunniford made a pot of tea in the same Belleek bone china and served sweet biscuit scones and melt-in-the-mouth butter tarts bursting with currants and glazed brown sugar. To this day, at Christmas time, I bake up a batch of Mrs. Hunniford's tarts. My own Irish tradition.

But times have changed, life is not as hard as it once was. In North America, my life eventually became more prosperous. These days Ireland is in a state of prosperity, second only to Finland in economic status. Eighty percent of Irish schoolchildren go on to attend college. Even in the 1980s, Irish people were still immigrating to England in search of work. Now this small island is a huge exporter of computer software and manufacturer of pharmaceuticals. The town of Ringaskiddy in County Cork provides thousands of jobs to people working in the Pfizer factory. Farming and family-run shops are becoming a rarity in this age of super highways, urban sprawl, electronic communication and easy-access mega stores.

Reminding myself that I'd met many working people in my weeks in Ireland, I realized that people who work for a living in Ireland weren't necessarily having Paula's rough time. Maude and John O'Connell, for example, have owned the mini-market shop in the quiet hamlet of Myrtleville, about fifteen miles from Cork City, for fifty years. Things certainly may have been tight for them in earlier years. Maud, a neat, no-nonsense woman, now in her late seventies, had been a hotel maid; her husband, John, had been a farm laborer. Eventually they managed to put a payment on the shop with its attached two-story house at the back, their pride very much in evidence in their large front garden with its verdant lawn and multiple varieties of blooming roses. Their three children were born and grew up in the Myrtleville house. Two are married and living in other towns— Kildare and Midlands—but forty-year-old Paul still lives at home and works at the shop.

Paul remembers an unspectacular childhood. He and his brother and sister had to work regular hours in the grocery shop and had a lot of fun and good times biking and making forts in the surrounding hills. When the city people came to stay in their summer homes, the city kids and the locals played together at the beach, making rafts and primitive dinghies. The family ate unvaried meals of spuds boiled in their skins with lots of bacon and cabbage, with one major exception. During

July, August, and September, they all caught mackerel, an oily, bony fish, right off the beach.

He laughs, "We'd fry it up for breakfast, lunch and dinner!"

Paul O'Connell isn't sure that the new Irish prosperity is all for the good. "We'd have Christmas once a year and be glad for what we got. Now the kids have Christmas every week, new gadgets all the time. The teenagers have loads of money, no respect, and they're just out for a good time."

In Buckley's, a pub in the peaceful town of Crosshaven, I met Noreen, a round-bodied barwoman with an unworried smile. She casually commented about going to Mallorca in Spain for their holiday two weeks earlier. Later, at the quiet, crescent-shaped beach near my Myrtleville B&B, I encountered Noreen, her husband Jack, a house painter, and their web-footed Labrador retriever. Every day until November the three of them go for their morning swim, diving into water that can't be more than fifty-five degrees Fahrenheit. Aside from the relative luxury of a holiday in Spain, I suspect that these two do what they want to do, with a grin, in the face of economic ups or downs.

I admired their stamina and the way they happily braved the icy waters. It exemplified the spirit of Roddy Doyle's characters, a spirit I'd come to think of as Irish. In a way, I'd found Paula. I found people infused with an unfamiliar prosperity, still sticking to tradition and their down-to-earth good nature and grit. On this beautiful green island, now the Celtic Tiger, the old ways of Ireland are changing, but the old verve remains and, truly, it is grand.

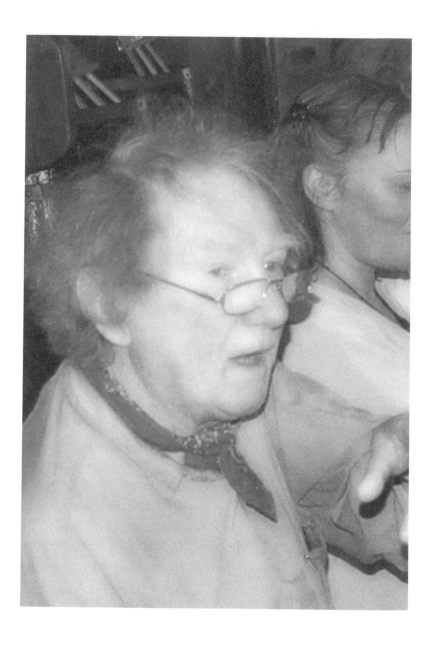

High Mass at the Spaniard Inn

Denise Altobello

"   id ya' write anythin' today, Desmond?"
"Aye, love, I did. But 'tis the hour now of High Mass."

We are sitting in wait at the Spaniard Inn, a pub in Kinsale, as her poet-in-residence, Desmond O'Grady, steps inside at the crack of day—eleven o'clock. Old blue eyes teasing, white blond hair flowing, bushy eyebrows flying like kite tails in a breeze, Desmond is every student's picture of an aging poet in his pink trousers and brightly colored scarf wound tight around his well-worn neck.

The server at the tap smiles her affection at his slightly stooped, but still commanding figure. "It's been a while since we've seen you, yes it has."

"Aye, lass," he returns in a voice, seasoned, though weakened, by whiskey and years. "Since beyond the misty space of a thousand years."

But this morning, lucky for me, the Spaniard Inn's altar has beckoned Mr. O'Grady.

This dreamy encounter is my lyrical introduction to one of Ireland's natural treasures. A recovering Catholic from New Orleans, the land of dreamy dreams celebrated in history and legend for its notorious saints and sinners, a thrill of irreverence stirs within my blasphemous soul as Desmond's wicked wit entices me into his version of High Mass. High priest of the Spaniard Inn, he nourishes my spirit with tales of Ireland's poetic icons past and present, as well as one about an intriguing tryst with the Emerald Isle's most provocative *femme fatale*— the mythical Sheela-na-gig. A congregation of fifteen, we disciples break bread together around a long, wooden table scarred by a century of blarney and pints, devouring the poet's words with a hunger worthy of the original evangelists.

Desmond O'Grady is surely not the first to choose a neighboring watering hole for communion and inspiration. Across the ocean, in the years before hurricane Katrina, Herb, my daughter-in-law's father, used to religiously meet with his buddies every Sunday morning for a private mass at Wimpies, a bar downriver from New Orleans. Although most of the wives chose to attend more traditional services in the many Irish, German and French churches dotting the Mississippi River's banks, these men found a richer spiritual sustenance in the music, laughter, banter and beer at Wimpies.

"As my old friend Ezra Pound always reminded me when I

was just a young poet, 'you must eat well and always have
something to show for it,'" Desmond is saying. "So I come here
for a pint and some *craic*," the Irish equivalent of Louisiana's
"*laissez les bons temps rouler!*" Such was the Gospel according
to Ezra Pound. Inspiration at the Spaniard Inn really does come
from on high. We God-fearing bar hoppers at home look no
higher for wisdom than to Fats Domino on the jukebox, dutifully preaching of the wages of sin and reminding us that "the
sun never shines in Whisky Heaven."

I had learned that morning that Desmond has seventeen
volumes of poetry to his credit. Most assuredly, he has blessings
to show for his years of devotion to the Spaniard Inn and other
such churches across the lands he has traveled. Founding member of the European Community of Writers, our luncheon cele-
brant widens the ken of his faithful not only with his own lyrics
but also with his moving translations of both Greek and Arabic
verse.

For more than an hour, Desmond weaves his enticing spell
around us. I lean in closer to the cherubic face with the Irish
blush as he recounts tales of his travels and friendships with the
seraphim of the arts: Ezra Pound, Samuel Beckett, John
Berryman, Pablo Neruda, even Pablo Picasso. A devotée of
these icons for nearly four decades, I scarcely touch my rapidly
congealing goat cheese salad, determined to glean as much as I
can from his mellifluous but often cryptic Irish syllables.
Periodically, he pauses, shakily places a morsel of brown bread
on his tongue and bends his head to the vessel holding his dark

Murphy's. My rapture is interrupted by a vision burning with sacrilege. Is Desmond really lifting the glass with reverence, or is my annoyingly loyal Catholic prism distorting this image?

Just as I swat this thought away, one of the other writers asks, "Would you like a bit of this wine, Desmond?"

"Oh no," he points to his ale, lengthening and opening his o's in the "oh so Irish" way of County Cork. "Never mix the grape with the grain."

"Hey," I think, "if this is High Mass, then Father Desmond is twisting the rules for his own pleasure. Can true communion even occur without wine? Certainly not in my religion of drink—not in the churches I frequent nor at the table I set. I decide that the old poet surely has his fluent tongue set firmly in his cherubic cheek, and I settle back into my role as one of the faithful. He preaches for a while about his times as a teacher and of his conviction that the artist should "teach to travel and then travel to amuse and feed the muse." A long-time teacher whose wanderlust was placed on hold for too many years, I hush my rarely silent inner voice at last as Desmond reminisces about his time in Paris where he lived above the famed Shakespeare & Company bookstore and accompanied "Sam to the opening night of *Godot*." Dear God, this man has lived among the altars where I have worshipped for most of my heathen life. Paris, Beckett, bohemians, rebellion. The very pillars of my unholy faith.

"*My Alexandria*," he brogues, "is my newest work." A voice from further down the table interjects, "Would you please tell us a bit about your years in Egypt?"

"Cairo is a slum," he retorts, "except for the Sphinx, of course, and her inviting orifice."

He's done it again. With a simple double-entendre, Desmond lightens the mood with his dark and enticing wickedness. The comment also leads to another mystery of the Irish faith, the significance of Sheela-na-gig, the erotic, yet grotesque image of the hag squatting and opening her own special orifice found embellishing walls of Norman churches throughout Ireland and England. "Desmond, have *you* ever encountered Sheela-na-gig?"

"Aye, lass, I have. She's not a good woman. She's dangerous to men. I met her one night. She tried to seduce me. 'O'Grady,' she says. 'I'm tough; I live on Tough Alley. The further down you get, the tougher it gets. And I'm the last house.'" Desmond shakes his head in remembrance of his near escape from the mighty clutches of one of mythology's most fearsome feminine archetypes, his eyes twinkling with delight at our eruption of laughter at his salacious innuendo.

This sounds to me a bit like the warnings the priests used to give Catholic schoolboys at home. Despite this irritating reminder, the lure of Sheela's dangerous invitation to Desmond tickles my fancy and whets my appetite for more.

Matthew Geled, the Kinsale poet and bookseller, who has gathered with us around our table on this cold and windy summer day, has brought a stack of Desmond's books. The conversation takes a more poignant direction as Desmond, while signing them, notes how many of us have selected his translations of *Kurdish Poems of Love and Liberty*. His voice softens as he explains the fundamental connection he sees between the traditions of Irish and Kurdish literature.

"There are five loves, you see, in both traditions." He raises one gnarled finger at a time and enumerates: "First, there is love of the land. Second, the country—Ireland, for me, you know. Then, love of church. Next, love for mother, and finally," he raises his head, his blue eyes looking out from under the wild nest of brows. I hold my breath awaiting the greatest commandment of all. "Love of the muse." Only the scratching of our scribbling pencils disturbs the hush of the moment. Chuckling at our collective piety, Desmond once again deftly lifts the veil of transcendence and plops us back into the realm of the Irish trickster with one simple sentence: "You noticed that I said *muse*, not *wife*, did you? *Wife* is a four-letter word, you know." His unkempt brow reaches in my direction.

Once again, my instinctive anger at Catholicism's paradoxes burns hotly. *Honor motherhood, sure. But set upon all women the impossible standard of the miraculously virgin mother. And lay blame for original sin at the feet of Eve and her influence on the otherwise innocent Adam.* As though reading my thoughts, Father Desmond winks in my direction and shrugs his hunched shoulders. My mental rail against biblical history subsides as I realize that he's just windin' us again like a master angler on the high seas.

I am still ruminating on my simultaneous delight and indignation when lunch comes to an end. We keep Desmond from reaching into his pocket as we tally the bill and fill the final collection plate. We assure him that we are all honored for him to have been our guest. In what I have come to recognize as his inimitable tease, he expresses his appreciation and adds: "This is good. Women are always supposed to pay the check. *I've never really learned how to write one.*"

We communicants answer with a final chortle and a flurry of handshakes around and across the table. Desmond rises, waves his weak and green-sleeved hand to dismiss his flock, and delivers his Irish blessing,

May you have warm words on a cold evening,
A full moon on a dark night,
And the road downhill all the way to your door.

THE GARDEN ISLE

SANDRA BRACKEN

Traveling in southern Ireland two years ago, I felt I was in a monochromatic painting that might have been entitled "Variations on the Color Gray." It was as if a translucent curtain had been lowered and the colors of the world beyond were pale, incomplete versions of themselves. Walking the lanes near our rented cottage there was little green to be seen. Fields of peat were turned over in rows, waiting to be harvested. Constant rain only muddied the view. Green, the distinctive color of Ireland was missing. Was what I had read an exaggeration? It was October, but was it always so dreary?

I have returned. It is early summer, a time of promise. Already the curtain of mist and rain is penetrated with rays of sun illuminating fresh colors.

It is my habit to begin the day walking, no matter where I

am. With my Ordinance Survey map tucked into my pocket (Cork #87), I have a choice of roads and it lessens the chance I'll get lost. The road in front of the B&B winds past the local beach and at the second turn, I am dazzled by an expansive view of the ocean. I intend to walk for an hour, but I'm stopped in awe of a massive shrub of St.-John's-wort which seems to have grabbed the scarce bits of sunshine and holds them out to cheer passers-by. It's the first moment I am sure that things will be different this time.

The land falls steeply down to waves breaking noisily on large boulders. Houses are perched on both sides of the road. Bushes of hydrangeas snug up against one another, lacecaps and mop heads of saturated magenta stand within fences of tall fuchsia shrubs. Clumps of agapanthus are breaking into bloom, a cerulean blue. Another hillside, to the west, is showy in yellow potentilla, primrose and santolina. Cultivated gardens tumble into the road joining the multitude of wild flowers including two valerians side by side, one white, the other pink, next to lavender and lambsear. Then I see a palm tree and remember that this coast is warmed by the Gulf Stream.

Looking across Ringabella Bay to the next headland, pasture land is divided into squares of green fields, each a different shade, as if laid out in all the greens from a paint box, celadon to viridian. It is a spectacular arrangement of greens, a demonstration of all its possibilities. I can't help but think that this view was created just for me because I didn't believe it existed.

Walking up the driveway to our B&B, there's a welcoming

mix of evergreen and blooming shrubs. I'm attracted to a mauve ceanothus in full bloom. I'm always looking for gardening ideas and zoom in on the striking dwarf maple between two hydrangeas, three shades of the color purple. It is the entry to a garden full of good ideas, as well as seeming to satisfy the needs of a discriminating chef. Three small trees—one an apple— seem to be thriving miraculously in a raised bed in front of a high stucco wall. In between each are roses, a colorful contrast to the gray wall. Below, a variety of herbs provide ground cover.

A pink and yellow honeysuckle climbs gracefully around the dining room door behind two dozen pots which comprise the kitchen garden. The largest contains a bay tree more than twenty years old. Other pots hold tomato and cucumber plants, more herbs, more edible flowers, mints, and flowers just for color or personal pleasure. One afternoon the owner walks with me through the garden and enthusiastically answers my questions. I mention the fig tree growing at the edge of the lawn. The fruit are large and perfectly shaped, but still green. I am secretly longing to be here in a month to sample one—or two. "We're in competition with the birds for those figs" she laughs, as if reading my mind. Her skills lie in the kitchen as well as the garden. If there are figs left, I imagine she will make fig jam or a sauce.

At the corner of the terrace is a low dish-like pot holding a small palm. Under it are clusters of heathers, azaleas, nasturtiums, pansies, and campanula. The owner explains, "I wanted something blooming every season." She is always trying out new plantings—a bougainvillea is waiting to go in the ground. "I move the pots around—some places are bare in winter." I can see she is aware of her garden view from the house just as I am.

I expected to sleep and eat here; I did not expect this miniature garden of Eden with its own soothing stream. I begin to realize just how many Edens might be growing here.

Several days later I am eager to explore our next destination, the garden of Lismore Castle. Luckily, our guide is Chris Tull, the head gardener. Despite impending rain, he cheerfully walks with us through a series of outdoor rooms comprising some of the seven-acre garden. It is thought to be the oldest in Ireland. I am awed by its impressive variety of magnolias, a stunning davidia, a Chilean myrtle, and the long herbaceous borders. And entering the grassy avenue lined with four-hundred-fifty-year-old yews, I am completely filled with the pleasure of strolling through another time, like Alice in Wonderland.

Chris sounds like an art historian as he thoroughly answers our questions about the sculptures placed throughout the garden. The most memorable for me is a ground piece by contemporary artist Richard Long entitled "Cornwall Slate Line." Stepping from turf onto the interlocking randomly shaped pieces of slate, I am aware that this path is not a normal one. It starts in the middle of the lawn, stops before reaching the other side and is too wide. I want to stand in the center of it and look for a long time in each direction, long enough to imbed on my mind's eye and heart the place of this moment. I wish for a pause in time. The group moves on.

I follow slowly to the parterre garden. The afternoon is

moving too fast. These more formal gardens are a soothing preliminary to the practical areas beyond: the orchard, vegetable gardens and greenhouses. There are questions about a vanilla tree. Adjacent to the greenhouses is an area planted with a half dozen varieties of penstemon. I'm wondering which varieties might be available at home, hoping all of them.

The grandeur of Lismore compares oddly to the simplicity of another site of unexpected beauty that we visit the following day. The lane approaching Drombeg Stone Circle is not manicured, rather it follows an ordinary hedgerow. Set in a ring of furze, bracken and brambles, these seventeen standing stones share a long pastoral view through adjacent farms to the sea in the distance. Everyone is compelled to touch the stones, feel their power. While the Stone Age circle casts its spell, I wonder if the others of my party notice the tiny wild daisies under our feet. The present overlaps the past in buttercups and clover, campion and thistle; they add their contribution, bits of color—pink and white, yellow and purple. In a site overshadowed with pre-historic mystery, the little wildflowers add a note of everyday reassurance and, in their own way, heighten my experience of this place.

I am surprised to find so many plants that have an air of familiarity. And to see them growing so lustily reminds me that their size and vivid colors are in sharp contrast to their paler cousins on the next western landfall three thousand miles away. They are one more aspect of this stunning island garden in summer; this is not the Ireland of my recollection. As Desmond

O'Grady, the celebrated Irish poet, said to us, "Ireland always brings surprises." That it does. I am grateful to be here as the Irish curtain rises to reveal a land of surprising beauty, color and overwhelming green.

A Culinary Trinity

Laurie McAndish King

Long before I was old enough to be introduced to the mysteries of yeast and asexual reproduction, I learned to bake brown soda bread from my Grandma Hayes. She stood nearly five feet tall, always straight and proud, had red hair and freckles that she hated, and strong, cool arms that I loved. I didn't realize it at the time, but Grandma also taught me about transformation: creating rich sustenance from the simplest of ingredients. Brown bread always reminds me of Grandma Hayes. A loaf of it requires whole wheat flour, sour milk, soda, a strong stirring arm, and not a whole lot more. A slice provides nourishment and comfort beyond compare.

Thirty-five years after my grandmother's death, I visited Ireland's County Cork, a land of rolling green hills and patchwork fields—much like the farmland in southern Iowa where my grandparents settled and I grew up—and was stunned to discover Grandma's brown bread in nearly every pub and restaurant in Cork. Many of these establishments guarded their recipes for it fiercely; I know, because I asked for it at pubs like the Overdraught, the Armada, and the Spailpin Fanac. They all served brown bread, along with another dark substance I quickly learned to love—stout. And by stout, I mean Guinness and Beamish and Murphy's.

I drink stout now, a form of dark beer. A pint at a time, and it needn't even be cold. My favorite is Murphy's, a lightweight among dark beers perhaps, but with quite a respectable bite. First I down the head—a dense, creamy layer that tickles my nose and situates itself staunchly on my upper lip, neither dripping nor evaporating like the foamy froth on American beer. Instead, it makes itself quite at home until I dare to wipe it away. Sometimes I do not bother. The brew itself has a quiet silkiness, artfully balanced by a sharp and toasty bite that fills the mouth, quenches the soul.

I think I could live on Irish beer and brown bread, so I decided to search out the best. At the Guinness brewery in Dublin I learned how stout is made with barley, hops, water and yeast. First, the barley is soaked in water, drained, and allowed to germinate. The resulting "malt" is roasted like coffee beans until it turns toasty brown; this gives the brew a rich, distinctive color and flavor. Hops are added for bitterness and aroma; then the concoction is mixed with pure, soft water and boiled. Next comes yeast, a rich source of protein and vitamins.

This is where the asexual reproduction comes in. After it is added the brew is held in darkness for several weeks to ferment—the yeast transforming barley sugar into carbon dioxide (carbonation) and alcohol—and so the stout's flavor can develop and mature.

That was an easy lesson. Local brown bread recipes proved harder to pin down. At the Bride View Bar in Waterford, Ann Marie, a fresh-faced lass with curly blond hair and a crisp white linen blouse, pleasantly refused to give away her brown bread recipe. She did divulge—in a conspiratorial whisper—that she uses a secret ingredient, and that it is not the cornmeal I had suspected. Gaby, our gracious proprietress at the Bellevue Bed & Breakfast in Myrtleville, confided that she includes treacle (syrup) and black walnuts in hers.

The short, round hostess at Jim Edwards' restaurant in Kinsale declined to give me her recipe, but cheerfully consented to explain the subtleties and secrets of other people's brown bread: "Some add an egg, some use sugar, white or brown, or extra treacle for more sweetness; some prefer sour milk over buttermilk; and be *certain* to sift the soda!" Another source—who declined even to be named—mentioned that if you line the loaf pan with buttered parchment, it will ensure that the crust stays moist, and the bread will keep for four or five days, rather than the usual one or two.

After my diligent investigation of brown bread and beer, I thought I understood a good portion of Ireland's rich, dark culinary heritage, but there was one more surprise for me: a breakfast of Clonakilty black pudding. Although it isn't really pudding, it *is* really black, and it is served in soft, sausage-like discs, each about an inch and a half in diameter and three-eighths of an inch thick, regularly studded with pale kernels of what turned out to be barley. The kernels had just enough bite that they each popped—a bit like caviar—under the tooth, after which the pudding was bulky enough to fill the mouth roundly, with a rich creaminess. The whole of it was perfectly seasoned, salty enough to compel another bite, and with just a tease of pepper, that came onto the tip of my tongue well after I had swallowed the rest, each morsel suggesting that another mouthful might very well be in order. What ultimately seduced me was the generous texture—the gentle pop, a creamy chew, and only then the peppery suggestion. This could easily become my favorite food, except for the fact of what it is: blood.

The *black* in black pudding is congealed pork blood, and I am nearly a vegetarian. So I nibbled at the stuff excruciatingly slowly, considering with each small bite—and in between bites, too—exactly *what* I was eating, and straining to taste an excuse to push the plate aside. The excuse never manifested; Clonakilty's black pudding is, in fact, delicious beyond description—a perfect comfort food.

And comfort has long been needed in Ireland. After all, it is a country whose inhabitants have endured much hardship and deprivation. I have often wondered about the mystery of Irish authors—Swift, Wilde, Joyce, Beckett, O'Brien and Doyle, to name a few greats—how these people, in a land invaded and oppressed for centuries, manage to produce such lyric laments. How do they create pleasure and nourishment from such a bitter history? Perhaps the darkness of their subjugation allowed pain to ferment into music and longing to transmute itself into poetry. It is not so different from yeast, rising in darkness from a single cell to form a rich source of sustenance.

Yeast was in Grandma Hayes' larder, and Yeats was in her library. I learned both their lessons well: In "Cuchulain's Fight with the Sea" Yeats seems to reveal some of the mystery behind Ireland's eloquent transmutations,

I only ask what way my journey lies
For He who made you bitter made you wise.

Wise indeed—in bread, in beer, in blood—an Irish trinity worth toasting.

FAERIES

CHRYSA TSAKOPOULOS

Ah, faeries, dancing under the moon,
A Druid land, a Druid tune!
—W.B. YEATS
"To Ireland in the Coming Times"

Mud tastes better than I had imagined. Slowly peeling my face from the lawn, I heard the blossoms whisper, desperately trying to suppress their laughter, "The only ones who saw you were the faeries." Pushing up from the root that had tripped me, I rose slowly to my knees, lost in a whirlwind of childhood stories of pixie adventures and the dull throbbing in my knocked elbow. As I began my quest on the Emerald Isle, my head overflowed with tales and legends of a world beyond this one, packed with mythical creatures laced with gossamer wings. The ethereal world in which these fabled beings lived seemed eternally distant yet strangely present. I arrived in Ireland on a mission to discover faeries, and I was lucky enough to encounter them.

My work began where many dignified pursuits do: the lush pages of books. Although many storytellers have similar depictions, my research showed that scholars to the present day fiercely debate the origins of faeries. The ancient Celts believed that faeries were the children of the god *Dagda* and the goddess *Danu* (sometimes referred to as *Anu*), the great mother goddess of all that roamed the worlds. The ancient inhabitants called the children of this union the *Tuatha de Danann* meaning the "children of Danu." Some of the *Tuatha de Danann*, also known as the *Sidhe*, built extraordinary palaces of crystal and gold in the hollow knolls and ancient burial grounds of Ireland, while others constructed castles of pearls and shells in the depths of the sea. The unwavering belief in faeries by the natives upon the arrival of Christianity to the island caused the Church to offer its own explanation. It proclaimed that these "creatures" were in fact angels that were too good for hell but not good enough for heaven. According to this theory, the position of the faeries between heaven and hell was due to their inordinate pride. Still others believed that it was due to their lack of engagement in God's war against Lucifer that determined their fate.

To me faeries transcended debate. I had donned faery wings

for countless Halloweens and hopped around like Tinkerbelle exploring the enchanted forest in my backyard. The magic did not fade with childhood. Many moonlit nights were spent devouring the pages of William Shakespeare's *A Midsummer Night's Dream,* which opened a new door to the *Tuatha de Danann.* I imagined myself with Titania lounging on Neptune's yellow sands and following Puck on his mischievous errands. I even memorized Shakespeare's Sonnet 154, which told of the chaste nymphs that stole cupid's arrows.

This current trip to Ireland had reawakened my love for faeries. In 1922, following the release of photographs depicting leaping leprechauns and twirling sprites, Sir Arthur Conan Doyle wrote *The Coming of the Fairies,* the scholar's sincere attempt to provide facts to support the mythology. Whatever their origin, I was convinced that faeries still danced upon the earth. And I was prepared to search.

My hunt began in the haze of semi-slumber as our bus pulled to a halt at an old gray stone gate. I stepped gingerly out of the vehicle, which now seemed oddly displaced in the serene environment. The gray towers of Lismore Castle pierced the cloudy sky, which that morning seemed unusually low. The Dukes of Devonshire, its owners, truly experienced Ireland in style. The structure appeared to have been drawn with a magical paintbrush against the silver sky. Slender vines slithered up the ash-colored stone walls. A circular tower jutted out from the side of the building. The entire edifice seemed enchanted.

Even more exquisite than the castle itself were the gardens.

A forest of green, deeper and more vibrant than I had ever seen, with brilliant fuchsia and glowing white flowers splashed upon the bushes, rolled down for acres. A gentle wind carried the sweet freshness of summer rain, mixed with the subtle tartness that comes with the realization of ephemeral life.

Our guide Chris Tull, the prime minister of the verdant expanse (head gardener, as he had introduced himself) ushered us through the herbage, shrubs and types of flora one could only imagine. My fellow writers and I passed by lofty magnolia trees whose blossoms perched softly upon their branches. Camellias lined the soft green path through which Tull directed us. To our sides, the soft soil was spritzed with rhododendron plants whose flowers had bloomed months before in unusually warm April sunshine. In the middle of the garden near the castle itself was an extraordinary sculpture by the artist Richard Long. Countless jagged-edged stones of gray, white and black had been fitted together as movable art. The artist provided the stones: the person who assembled them truly manipulated the power of the piece.

The most mystical part of the garden was the corridor of yew trees. The deep green conifers stretched up like fingers intertwining at the tips and sheltered those below from the rain that slipped from the clouds. The air hung thick, pulsing slowly from the breath of trees. It is believed by those in Lismore that this spot was the inspiration for Edmund Spencer's *The Faerie Queen*. If there really were faeries, I could think of no grander and more worthy place for them to waltz.

Slightly weary after the long walk, I spied a lovely blue bench under a tall tree and sat. Closing my eyes, I felt a soft touch on my hand. My mind saw a tiny creature clothed in a dress the color of starlight, skin as pale as water lilies floating on an inky lagoon on a moonless night. Layers of crimson hair spilled down her shoulders and her eyes shone violet in the evaporating sunlight. She danced gracefully on my palm. Slowly opening my eyes, my gaze fell on the green leaf that had cascaded down from the tree above into my imagination. Standing a bit unsteadily, I rejoined my fellow writers.

The next morning I pried myself from my cozy bed, slipped on my burgundy coat and turquoise rubber sandals and set off towards the coast. Wending my way past cows, mailboxes and taverns, I arrived at the rocky shoreline. A heavy fog crawled along the surface of the Atlantic Ocean and gigantic jagged black cliffs plunged into the frothy water. The earth quivered under my feet. A salty wind wafted across the path between the protruding slabs of stone. A palette of purple, lavender, gold, green and cream-colored rocks speckled with seashells and dried kelp swathed the shore. I imagined sliding under the surface of the water to the violet and silver walled castles whose towers glittered brilliantly and strolling along streets lined with crystal cobblestones and opal lampposts. If some faeries had built their palaces beneath the waves, then surely I could think of no spot more picturesque. Moving slowly away from the mothers and their children frolicking in the tide, I rested on a bed of smooth stones not far from the surf. Leaning my back against the serrated crag, the sound of the waves floated softly on the breeze.

My head drifted to the side and before me appeared a man the size of my index finger clad in green velvet trousers, his head crowned with red feathers. With hair as soft as goose down, his eyes glittered the sapphire color of the waves. His pomegranate lips parted as he hummed the soft tune of bliss. I opened my eyes, and brushed the grey feather from my aching knuckles.

Startled, I glanced to make sure no one had seen me. Gazing at the waves, I felt like Nick Bottom strutting around with an ass' head. Or perhaps I really was Titania, caressing an ugly donkey as all looked upon her and laughed. Silly fool. There were no palaces under the sea or cities in the hills. There's no tooth faery either. In the clear light of midmorning, I returned home, desperately fighting the growing doubts in my heart.

That night I tossed and turned for hours and hardly slept. Consumed by doubt and reservations, I contemplated the seemingly silly faery fantasies. My mind chastised my heart for its childishness. Even the great Sir Arthur Conan Doyle had believed in faeries, my heart pleaded, especially after examining the pictures and publishing a book on the subject. It would be revealed many years later, my mind taunted back, that the pictures which Doyle had so devoutly supported were in fact hoaxes. I fell asleep embarrassed.

I had yet to meet Sister Eily. She is one of the most remarkable nuns I have ever met. Unlike many devout religious followers who fail to recognize the great essence that binds together all the souls of the earth, Sister Eily understands the mysteries of the spirit. After spending many years teaching in Australia, her heart yearned for the Emerald Isle. She accompanied our group to a place where she had come to mourn the loss of her mother, a place of unspeakable electricity and magic. She led us to Drombeg Circle.

In the midday mist of the last day of June, little droplets of rain sailed down from the heavens and danced upon the dainty yellow flowers that surrounded the Drombeg Circle. Large slabs of gray silver rock protruded gracefully from the green and dampened soil. The stones themselves seemed soft to the touch—not like the cold and hard stones that buttress the roofs of countless houses of worship. These stones sang. They hummed of mysteries thousands of years old and of sacrifices once praised but now forgotten. They crooned of winds and storms that had crashed into the rolling hills and jagged cliffs of Erin and they chanted of eternal love and everlasting hope. But loudest of all, the stones welcomed. They welcomed dreamers, adventurers and those foolish enough to believe in the impossible. Yes, it was we who found comfort there. We the ramblers, the lovers, the fools.

There, the tears my heart wept for dreams dashed by doubt finally dried. For what Sir Arthur Conan Doyle and countless before him had known is that it's not what falls before the eyes nor slides through the mind that creates truth. Truth is found beyond the deep caverns and soaring zeniths of the soul, reached only through laughter, tears and encounters with the divine wherever it may show itself. At Drombeg Circle, the faeries certainly held their festivities. As Doyle once said, "there is nothing scientifically impossible, so far as I can see, in some people seeing that which is invisible to others." As the Irish earth speckled with faery footprints and tracks of *Sidhe* chariots rose before my eyes, I heard their faint pipes in the whistle of the wind.

Irish Breakfast

Annelize Goedbloed

Breakfast. The first meal of the day and a meal it is. We are in Ireland and a full Irish breakfast is supposed to "carry you through the day." It is said that when you are not able to finish, you will have been served a proper Irish breakfast. I shudder. Breakfast. Who sets the time for it? Who sets the time for daily activities anyway, be it office hours or for a nurse galloping into your hospital room? I strongly believe that almost all activities whether necessary, entertaining, or carnal can take place at any moment of the twenty-four-hour day. Only a few are restricted to either daylight or darkness.

The apparent consensus of the time for breakfast is seven in the morning. All of us are supposed to join *hey ho, hey ho*, when the sun rises or—as is more often the case in this country—when it's just trying to penetrate the fog over the sea, as the fishermen return from their night's catch, and seagulls enthusiastically trail behind waiting for their breakfast to be served. This fact dismays the traveling night person who is by definition allergic to morning, a time when she is still too weak to chew.

It's a sad truth that no one will applaud nor register any admiration when I, a night person, am still fit as a fiddle, working or entertaining at midnight. Nobody is dismayed when morning people turn into pieces of furniture after ten at night, eyes drooping like zombies. Yet, everybody will disapprove and complain when a night person is not up and on the go at dawn. It is pure discrimination.

But here I am, a Dutch woman and the only European in this group of American travel writers. All are well-educated, well-traveled, intensely motivated, intensely cheerful morning people. *Hey ho, hey ho.* They are of course all there, very much there, eager for the Irish breakfast. This amazing American intensity will sink into the bog of my early morning constitution.

But please note: Full Irish breakfast is NOT English breakfast. Don't dare make any remarks on your black tea suggesting that it tastes and looks just like English breakfast tea. No it is a *different blend entirely*, although Assam in it predominates just as in English breakfast tea. Don't ever get confused because you have bacon and eggs, tomato, mushrooms, potatoes and sausages—just like an English breakfast. Remember that these are all very, very Irish. The yolks are the sunniest, the butter, milk and cream are the tastiest, the bacon is the meatiest. Don't forget the black pudding, which is the bloodiest, and of course the dark bread, which is of the finest milled wheat. Your muesli is definitely Irish and so are your cornflakes even if they say Kellogg's. The pile of toast and marmalade is Irish as well. It should be stated, however, that the black pudding has barley in it, and that the coarse Irish brown soda bread is a treat. I believe they could also be recommended in an anti- hemorrhoid diet.

When in Ireland, never, but really never, confuse anything Irish with anything English. This is quite understandable in view of what the English have done to the Irish. In fact, these sensitivities should be taken into account in many countries in the world where great suffering has been inflicted by an occupying nation. For example, never ask for a Turkish coffee in Greece, although Greek coffee is identical, nor tell a Dutch person the language sounds so much like German.

In Ireland, the English gained full power over the country in the early sixteenth century, and with the institution of the "penal laws" almost all rights were denied to the Irish; the Catholic Irish were barred from the army, the navy, the law, commerce and from every civic activity. They couldn't vote, hold any office, nor purchase land, and all estates were held by the British. They couldn't attend schools, nor send their children to be educated abroad, and the Catholic faith was proscribed. The Irish people were thus oppressed, impoverished, degraded and debased. They were even sold as slaves. Their plight is reflected in the lines of this song:

If you had the luck to be Irish
you had to be sorry and wish you were dead
If you had the luck to be Irish
you had wished you were English instead.

Then, with the Great Irish Famine (1845-1851), things only got worse. The famine came with the potato blight and the massive failure of the staple crop of the poor Irish. Yet, although the government in London was aware of the crisis, it continued to export grain, meat and dairy from Ireland. Up to this day, there are those who accuse England of genocide. In 1916, the poet Patrick Pearse read a proclamation for the Irish rebels in which the Republic of Ireland was proclaimed. The revolt was, however, smothered, and it was not until after another rising (including civil war) in 1921 that Ireland was recognized as a Free State by England. At last, as recently as 1949, the Irish Republic was proclaimed. Meanwhile the country remained economically semi-dependant on England.

This changed completely after Ireland entered the European Common Market. Ireland has made an economic leap forward with the help of the European Union. Since wealth apparently boosts self-confidence, there are signs that the anti-English feelings are softening. But the memory of the Great Famine and its subsequent wave of hundreds of thousands of destitute people leaving the country is vivid.

Nowadays the economy is booming and Ireland is not exactly cheap. A B&B is definitely the best affordable place to be. The country is full of them. They are usually kept by nice people who enjoy having guests and do their utmost do give you an enjoyable stay.

In the dining room facing out to the sea, my tea is gently placed in front of me. Like thousands of others who now flock to Ireland for work or pleasure, first thing in the morning I am reminded that in Ireland today, the Great Famine is only a memory in this land of plenty.

Nowadays the first meal of the day is big enough to carry one through to evening: Irish Breakfast.

THE HOLY GROUND

GAIL STRICKLAND

And still I live in hopes to see the Holy Ground once more.
—IRISH SHANTY

"Fear the watery grave," Denise murmurs. Her long fingers weave together, clench, and release as we devour fresh mussels in wine and butter sauce at the Bride View Bar in Waterford. I asked to sit and talk with her after we visited the Cobh Heritage Centre. Formerly known as Queenstown, Cobh (cove), was the end of the train line, jumping off point of emigration for three and a half million men, women and children during the Great Famine. I am overwhelmed with the memory of the photographs I saw in the museum of parents who waved farewell from weathered wooden docks holding back their tears. It seemed to me their captured smiles held a bittersweet knowing that their role was to hold their fear and wait for their children and their children's children to return.

The Irish left family and loved ones behind who said farewell with the utmost hope, but also with the utmost loss. Many who moved on to new lives were lost to those left behind forever. Most of the Irish never returned. Many were never heard from again. How do any of us wait on the shore and hope for the return of someone we love, whether it's a reprieve from natural disaster, disease, emigration or war? How do we wait and not lose hope? How do we cope with fear?

Denise's piercing blue eyes and dark lashes settle in a gentle face framed by chestnut hair drawn back with a wide leopard-print band. Red lips smile and worry at the same time. I look carefully at the tightness surrounding them and worry how the museum's story of the plight of the Irish refugees has affected her.

With a shrug of her shoulders she admits that she left the museum to settle herself before going back in, but that she was okay. I didn't need to worry.

"In New Orleans, you have an attic and you have life pre-servers," Denise tells me, "Really, when a new baby is born, you go out and buy a cigar to celebrate and you buy a life preserver. If you don't and you stay through a hurricane, you're a damn fool."

Is that the secret? A cigar to celebrate and a life preserver to be safe? It's a tricky balance, or at least it has been in my life. If I worry too much about safety, I forget to celebrate. If I celebrate too much, I forget to stay safe. I laugh at my constant confu-sion. Maybe the secret is to have an attic to keep it all together.

I admire the Irish way. During the Famine, when family members emigrated hoping for a better life, the families staying behind held wakes, "American Wakes" they called them, as if their family member or friends had died. For those departed for the New World might as well have departed for the Great Beyond. Families pooled the meager food they had and danced and sang. I am amazed at the incredible ability of the Irish to find joy in the midst of sorrow.

When I walked through the Cobh Heritage Centre and read the devastating numbers of Irish lost through emigration and disease, I knew the statistics did not tell the whole story. Between 1858 and 1950, over six million adults and children emigrated from Ireland. Five thousand orphan girls were sent from workhouses to Australia as domestic help. Three and a half million people emigrated from 1855 to 1920 alone. Of those who did not emigrate, one and a half million died of cholera and starvation as the potato crop turned black and putrid year after year. Other Irish crops continued to go over-seas for profit with no one helping the starving farmers in the same way that elders in New Orleans waited in attics and rooftops after hurricane Katrina for help that arrived too late.

The figures I read attempted to explain the magnitude of the loss, but what did they really mean? What did they explain to the children whose father could no longer pay the rent while the absentee English landlords burned their cottages so they could not return? To a mother whose young sons left for Australia or New York or Canada often to die in the hold of a "coffin" ship from cholera or dysentery or simply to disappear into the vast maw of a distant continent? Would they find help in the New World? A home? A job? A way to survive that no longer existed in their homeland? Today four million Irish live in Ireland and 40 million live abroad.

Ireland lost so much that its loss can never be counted in numbers on a page or a pamphlet in a museum. It can only be comprehended, breathing and alive, in the birth of a new grandchild who will never know her grandparents or the farm where they live, where the stories sprout like thistles in a field gone fallow.

"Oh this is *The Cove Song*," the fiddle player's mother, Marguerite Cullinane, tells me later that week as we sit together with her husband at a small round table at Buckley's, a pub in Crosshaven, and listen to their young daughter play with some of the finest musicians I have ever heard.

"It's about the Holy Ground you see," her husband adds.

"What's the Holy Ground?" I ask, having never heard the term before.

He looks off into a far corner of the busy pub. His face flushes with reverence and awe as if he had been swept up and carried to a distant shore altogether. When he finally answers, he whispers, "*Cobh. Cobh* is the Holy Ground. The place where so many left Ireland."

That is the first time I hear Cobh described as the Holy Ground, but after he explains it to me, I hear it everywhere. I find an old sea shanty in an Irish folk song book called "The Holy Ground." When I ask Michael, our taxi driver, about

Cobh, "Oh, the Holy Ground," is his answer, a response I will hear time and again. Everyone I ask about Cobh gives me the same answer, and they never utter the words without going deep within to a pool that is their past and their hope for the return of loved ones—loved ones who seldom returned home. Each inward gaze, disconnected from whatever liveliness surrounds them—a pub, taxi, restaurant—is like an empty chair left waiting at their kitchen table.

A few days later on the bus touring southern Ireland, I talk with Sister Eily, and begin to fully understand how those departed never faded to mere memory. Sister Eily is a feisty, red-haired Irish Catholic nun. She sits in front of me and tells stories about her family, whispering her last story to me, a memory of the final days with her aging mother. There were tears in her mother's eyes, as she lay in bed resting, and Sister Eily asked her mother if she was uncomfortable or needed something.

"No," her mother answered in a voice frayed and worn. "I'm thinking of the day Gulann (her younger sister) went to go to Cobh and I made her that gray coat." Wearing her gray coat, Gulann left Ireland. Many years later, she returned.

I return home to California, but the memories of Ireland's losses haunt me. It is difficult for me to put the mass emigration into words, to hold onto their loneliness and fear. Sitting in the comfortable Adirondack chair in my garden, coffee mug in hand, I think one more time about something Denise told me.

"We live in fear of the next storm," she had admitted that

day we shared lunch, but she didn't dwell long on their worry. Instead, she told me a simple story I think will stay with me the rest of my life.

"My great-grandmother, she was Irish, gave me an old trunk when I was fourteen—a black trunk with wood straps that was my hope chest. I stored my books in it at the foot of my bed when I was in college." When Denise's son called to tell her that he had bought the ring to propose to his love, his "sweet Melissa," Denise went out right away to buy cake pulls for an engagement present.

"What are cake pulls?" I had no idea, but the name intrigued me.

She explained that good luck charms are put inside the wedding cake and all the unmarried close family members get a chance to pull on a ribbon and extract the silver charm from the cake. She gave Melissa her trunk for a hope chest and put the charms inside to save them for their wedding. The trunk was stored in Denise's sister's attic shortly before hurricane Katrina hit. After the storm, Denise's mother, son, and brother donned masks and waders to return to the flooded house and though the trunk had totally disintegrated in the muddy water, her mother poked around with her cane and stabbed the mud where that chest had been until she came up with the cake pulls.

"We used those cake pulls in their wedding cake."

I begin to see a pattern. Sew a gray coat for warmth. Extract the cake pulls from the storm's wreckage for luck. Whatever I do, create something for the future. Don't dwell on the past and live with fear watching over my shoulder. I pick up my drained coffee mug and walk inside to begin this story.

WINEGEESE

BARBARA J. EUSER

They flew from Ireland with a specific purpose in mind. Unlike the hundreds of thousands who fled Ireland in successive waves following the Great Famine and political disruptions, seeking a better life wherever opportunity could be found, the Winegeese knew where they were going. They sought opportunities in the lucrative wine trade and headed to the source of great French wine: Bordeaux.

Probably introduced by the Phoenicians, wine has been appreciated and highly valued in Ireland for over two thousand years. Perhaps because grapevines could not be successfully cultivated in Erin's overcast climate, wine achieved a particular status as a rare commodity.

In the time of the Phoenicians, wine production had spread from its origin in the Caucasus region to the Mediterranean basin. The Greeks, in particular, developed various strains of wine grapes. Together, the Greeks and Phoenicians spread these vines all the way to the Atlantic coast.

Indefatigable traders, the Phoenicians opened a route from the Mediterranean across today's France, through the Carcassonne Gap, down the Garonne River to the Bay of Biscay. From there, they traveled north along the coast, reaching Ireland and Cornwall from the Celtic Sea. The Phoenicians brought amphora of wine. They took back Irish implements and ornaments and valuable Cornish tin.

Feasting at the great courts of ancient Ireland was renowned. During the fifth through seventh centuries, the central seat of authority was at Tara, where the High Kings resided. In the poem "Tara of the Kings," from *The Grey Feet of the Wind*, Cathal O'Byrne describes such a feast,

> *The tables groaned beneath the mighty weight*
> *Of ponderous vats of rare and precious wines,*
> *And carcases of oxen roasted whole,*
> *Methers of foaming mead went gaily round*
> *From lip to lip, and friend and foe alike*
> *Ate, drank, and quaffed their brimming cups,*
> *Forgetting for the moment every wrong*
> *That ever held them sundered. Such the Law.*

Centuries later, wine was used as a medium of taxation. In the ninth century, the Vikings developed the port towns of southern Ireland: Cork, Waterford, Limerick, Wexford and Dublin. According to Ted Murphy, in his book *The Kingdom of Wine*, in the eleventh century, "the tribute system existed in Ireland and the Vikings of Limerick paid an annual tribute to King Brian Boru at his palace in Kincora on the Shannon, which consisted of a ton of wine for every day in the year." Translated into modern day seventy-five centiliter bottles of wine, that is one thousand five hundred and thirty-six bottles of wine for every day in the year. No wonder wine flowed freely in the king's banquet halls.

The connection between Ireland and Bordeaux drew closer in the twelfth century. In 1159, King Henry II received the title "Lord of Ireland" from Pope Adrian IV and, with it the Pope's blessing to invade the island. His Anglo-Norman army invaded Ireland and ultimately established control over much of the country. King Henry II's many territories included his wife Eleanor of Aquitaine's dowry, Bordeaux and many of the other wine-growing regions of France. Geraldus Cambrensis, a member of King Henry II's entourage, wrote in *The Topography of Ireland* in 1177, "Imported wines, however, conveyed in the ordinary commercial way, are so abundant that you would scarcely notice that the vine was neither cultivated nor gave its fruit there. Poitou out of its own superabundance sends plenty of wine, and Ireland is pleased to send in return the hides and animal skins of flocks and wild beasts."

The new Anglo-Norman establishment added its demand for wine to that of the traditional Gaelic chieftains. Wine trade with France flourished and Ireland itself became a center of wine trade. In 1412, the Vintage Fleet comprised some one hundred and sixty vessels plying to and fro from Bordeaux. It included five Irish ships, three from Kinsale and two from Dublin.

Wine was enjoyed at all levels of society. It was not limited to the upper classes. In 1735, George Berkeley in *The Querist* wrote that "while in England many gentlemen with one thousand pounds a year never drank wine in their houses, in Ireland this could hardly be said of any who had one hundred pounds a year."

But flourishing trade itself attracts taxation. By the sixteenth century, heavy duties were imposed by the English on the importation of wine into Ireland. The independent Irish countered by developing their own "free trade" in wine—known to the English Crown as smuggling. In an effort to stem free trade, the British government enacted legislation that recognized only certain cities where wine could legally enter the country. Among these were Cork City and Kinsale. In Kinsale, Desmond Castle became the Customs House and through it passed great quantities of imported wine. Today Desmond Castle houses the International Museum of Wine. Cork City wine families of note included Roache, Morrogh, Gallwey, Lawton and McCarthy. Descendents of these families were among the first Winegeese— Irish who emigrated to France to trade in wine.

Even for the merchants who profited from their privileged position in an approved port city, the restrictive legislation was burdensome. Added to the tumultuous political situation in

Ireland in the seventeenth and eighteenth centuries, it inspired up-and-coming youth to seek their fortunes elsewhere. Bordeaux, the source of some of the best French wines imported in Ireland, was an attractive destination.

Abraham Lawton of County Cork was one of the most successful Winegeese. Establishing the wine brokerage house of Tastet and Lawton in Bordeaux in 1739, he became an outstanding leader in the wine trade. He has been described as "one of the most influential figures in the wine history of Bordeaux," and "all powerful."

As foreigners, the Winegeese were prohibited from carrying out their trade within the city limits of Bordeaux. So they built their warehouses and homes along the Quai des Chartrons. Due to the wealth they created, the Chartronnais district became more beautiful than the city center. Irish traders shipped wine to Ireland and Ireland shipped back salted beef and butter. Eventually, Winegeese married into local wine-producing families and purchased vineyards of their own. They became part of some of the most renowned names in Bordeaux wines: Chateau Lynch-Bages, Chateau Latour, Chateau Leoville-Barton, Chateau Phelan-Segur, Chateau Siran, Chateau MacCarthy (now part of Chateau Haut-Marbuzet), Chateau Giscours and Chateau d'Yquem (McMahon family). Some Winegeese families, for example, the Johnstons maintain their presence on the Quai de Chartrons to this day: Nathaniel Johnston of Armagh founded Nathanial Johnston et Fils, now run by brothers Denis, Archibald and Ivanhoe Johnston.

Other seventeenth and eighteenth century Winegeese of note included Thomas Barton of County Fermanagh, Peter Mitchell of Dublin, Patrice MacMahon of Limerick, James Lynch of Galway, Bernard Phelan of Clonmel, and Denis McCarthy of Cork.

In 1787, Thomas Jefferson followed the ancient Phoenician trade route from the Mediterranean to the Garonne River and thus to the Bay of Biscay and the Atlantic. Unlike the ancient route, however, Jefferson made the voyage on a barge towed along the *Canal des Deux Mers*, also known as the Canal du Midi. Pierre Paul Riquet masterminded the building of the canal and the reservoirs that maintain its water supply. The Canal was completed in 1681, shortly following Riquet's death, and added considerably to the prosperity of Bordeaux, located where the Garonne River enters the Atlantic. During his trip along the Canal, Jefferson sampled local wines and kept notes in his journal on his favorites. When he arrived in Bordeaux, Jefferson was advised by a member of the Lawton family regarding wines to purchase for his *cave* in Paris. Following his return to the United States, Jefferson introduced George Washington to the wine of Bordeaux and purchased cases of wine for both of them, to be delivered by ship from Bordeaux to America.

The Johnston family developed the American connection, sending a representative to the United States in 1807. The trip was a commercial success and Winegeese Nathanial Johnston and Fils entered the New World. Ireland maintained its position as an entrepôt of wines: many of the wines shipped from Bordeaux passed through Ireland on their way to America.

Other Winegeese entered the New World as growers and traders. Dominic Lynch, with Galway roots, became a wine merchant in New York in 1785. He imported chateau-bottled wines from France and Madeira wine from that island.

Bernard MacMahon was born in Ireland in 1775. At twenty-one, he emigrated to the United States and established a horticultural center near Philadelphia. Although wine grapes were not being grown commercially in the United States at that time, MacMahon conducted pioneering experiments grafting vines. He also advocated hybridization as a way to develop vines suitable for the American climate. His advice proved correct and hybridization and grafting are standard practices throughout the world today.

James Concannon, born in the Aran Islands, purchased property in Livermore Valley, California in 1883, and planted a vineyard intending to make wine for the Catholic Church. He traveled to France and purchased root stock from the McMahon's Chateau d'Yquem, which he brought back and planted in Livermore. In 1889, Concannon traveled to Mexico and obtained a concession from the Mexican government to sell grape stock to local vintners. In five years, Concannon shipped millions of cuttings to Mexican growers, greatly impacting Mexican viticulture.

Wineries in California with Winegeese connections include Christopher Buckley's Ravenswood; Dan Gainey's Gainey

Winery; Bob Travers' Mayacamas Vineyards; Jack Cakebread's Cakebread Cellars; Robert Foley's Robert Foley Vineyards; Michael Collins' Limerick Lane Cellars; Jim Barrett's Chateau Montelena; Molly Chappellet's Chappellet Winery; Francis Mahoney's Carneros Creek Winery; and Mike Lee's Kenwood Vineyards.

Winegeese also traveled Down Under. Samuel McWilliam of Northern Ireland emigrated to Australia in 1857. With the planting of his first vineyard in 1877, he established McWilliams Wines, still producing wine today. The region he opened to viticulture is known as the Riverina, which accounts for two-thirds of wine production in New South Wales and nearly one-quarter in all of Australia.

The Cullen family, descended from a Wexford County Clarke who arrived in Australia in the eighteenth century, opened the Margaret River as a wine-producing region.

The Murphy family arrived in Australia from Cork in the 1860's. They established Trentham Estates in New South Wales in 1909. Murphy family members continue to run the business.

Other Winegeese flew as far as New Zealand, South Africa and Chile, developing vineyards and the wine trading businesses as they settled in their new homes.

But the story does not end with emigration. Ireland, which historically was not a wine-producing country, has become one. In 2000, the European Commission listed Ireland as a wine producer. The change has been brought about by work related to that of Brian MacMahon, one of the Winegeese who, in 1796, emigrated to the United States. The work MacMahon pioneered in the hybridization of grape varieties has continued. In 1964 in Czechoslavkia, Professor V. Kraus successfully crossed the varieties Zarya Severa and St. Larent to produce the Rondo grape. According to Irish wine writer Tomas Clancy, the Rondo grape "matures early and is resistant to frost and the harsh Irish climactic conditions. It ripens well in Irish summers and produces a pretty deep ruby red wine with a velvety, almost merlot-wash."

The Rondo grape is now being grown successfully in Ireland by David Llewellyn at his Lusk vineyard outside Dublin. In addition to his Rondo red wine, Llewellyn produces a popular sauvignon blanc. In the south, in Counties Waterford and Cork, credible wines are also being produced. Blackwater Valley Vineyard produces several thousand bottles of Reichensteiner white wine yearly. Longueville House Hotel produces just enough Reichensteiner and Muller Thurgau white wine to serve at its restaurant. Thomas Walk Vineyard near Kinsale grows the Amurensis grape, known for its durability in cold weather and named for the Amur River in northern China. Its red wine has been described as a "light Beaujolais." The Irish vineyards are nascent, and promising.

The Winegeese left Ireland to engage in the business of wine. They may now be able to begin the long migration home.

LÍMERÍCK GÍTY

❦

for Jack Donovan

Christmas blazed a bundle of bonfires.
Carousers jumped off bridges for bets
and the City of the Broken Treaty
drifted towards an unknown distinction
up and down the River Shannon.
Along the Flag of All Nations Street
a shadow moved on every threshold
in mysterious inviting relief.
Drawn blinds. No heat from
gaping fireplaces. Flowers
withered in their vases. Occasionally,
in the isolated suffocation
of those blank days,
an incomprehensible vision dawned.

But cautiously, scarcely daring
consideration. Buttoned up,
it brooded about in the rain
pelting up the river.
I believed we were possessed,
unwilling to recognize ourselves
in the dirty mirror
of our own on the forbidden docks,
my twentieth century—the real
not our politico-clerical century—
rode at anchor. Prepared to sail.

after Anna Akhmatova

—DESMOND O'GRADY

Dancing the Irish Polka

M.J. Pramik

"We ❤ Polski" boasted the sign on the crusted red bricks of an anonymous storefront on O'Connell Street around the corner from Eden Quay and the River Liffey, Dublin, one drizzly June morning.

"Polish spoken here," glittered the only notice in another Dublin shop window on Parliament Street.

On my recent quest to Ireland to discover the modern Irish soul, I did not expect to find descendants of my Polish forbearers populating the Emerald Isle. Apparently newly affluent Ireland has become the prime destination of hard-working Poles unhappy about the slow paced, still-in-transition Polish capitalism.

Steeped in Polish culture from birth in the eastern Ohio hamlet of Maynard, settled by Poles, Czechs, Slovenians and a few random Italians, the proverbial Irish surprise slugged my

71

psyche. Everywhere I walked I encountered Poles flooding the streets of not only Dublin but all of Eire. In the rebel southwest County Cork, many a native Corkonian lad has wedded many a Polish lass over the past decade.

Within the last fifteen years, the economy of the Celtic Tiger beckoned hundreds of international companies to set up operations. Low taxes and other fertile dispensations lured pharmaceutical and biotechnology companies, manufacturing and telecommunications industries. Close on the tail of this new prosperity, like dolphins and whales foraging after herring off the Irish coast, hundreds of thousands of immigrants set sail for the land of Erin. The Irish media reflects this change with new publications—three Polish (*Polska Gazeta, Sofa, Polski Express*), three African (*Eye, Bold and Beautiful, Xclusive*), two Lithuanian (*Lietuvis, Saloje*), two Chinese (*Shining Emerald, Tiao Wang Magazine*) and one each catering to the country's Russians (*Nasha Gazeta*), Latvians (*Sveiks*), Filipinos (*Filipino International*), and Pakistanis (*Pakistan Times*).

Most of Ireland's new "huddled masses" arrived from Eastern European countries. The majority, it seems, hail from Poland. Polish workers are ubiquitous. Friend Joanna related that when she checked the Internet in the Belfast public library, the Google default promptly appeared in Polish!

Poles. They are recognizable everywhere in Ireland: blond, with pale blue or deep brown eyes, fine features, a touching demeanor, and—I sensed—a sadness at being the "other."

"Are you Polish?" I asked.

Blond and upright in his well-fitted suit, the night clerk at Dublin's Trinity Capital Inn did not sound Irish. He answered my probing with a clipped certainty and an interesting, definitely non-Irish, linguistic twist.

"Ya, sure," was his direct reply, much like my father's terse, no nonsense retorts to my youthful queries. The young man explained that he was a computer engineering student taking time off from a Polish university.

"It's very difficult in Poland right now. The government is moving too slow in economic matters. Even a doctor cannot make an adequate income. Here, in Ireland, one can earn enough to live." He had spent the past year and a half working the nightshift at this Irish hotel directly across from Trinity College.

Poland, without any natural borders to protect its countryside and identity, harvests a people who emigrate to survive, a characteristic they share with the Irish. All four of my grandparents left their green rolling hills of southwestern Poland for similar landscapes in Ohio and Pennsylvania at the dawn of the twentieth century. They bid farewell to mother, father, and siblings, like myriads of Irish sailing to America from Cork harbor, never to see their loved ones again.

Today, many Poles in Ireland perform service sector jobs: shop girls selling Irish sausages, waitresses struggling with an Irish menu in a unique English accent, and au pairs in middle class Irish homes nurturing children for six to twelve months—work the newly affluent Irish gladly hand off.

Googling the Internet I found "vaveena.com, the complete

survival guide to living and working in Ireland," a website list-
ing science, medicine, and engineering jobs in Polish. It also
posted a host of unsavory sounding positions as well. "Party
Girl" did not have a long job description. It did not need one.

According to Polish Ambassador to Ireland Witold Sobkow,
the Polish adore Ireland and revere it as a land of hospitality
and beauty.

"[The Polish] people love Irish music, dancing, Guinness,
and whiskey. We have Irish pubs in Poland, we celebrate St.
Patrick's Day," said Ambassador Sobkow in an interview. He
also noted that Irish owners lease land to Polish farmers.
Bicultural marriages occur each year, usually a Polish girl and
an Irish boy plighting their troth.

Currently, it's estimated that some 250,000 to 400,000 Poles
have relocated to the Emerald Isle, recently displacing Chinese
as the largest minority. As in many courtships, the Irish-Polish
relationship had a rocky beginning. On May 1, 2004, any person with a red European Union (EU) passport could traverse
the EU countries and work without a permit. Soon, newspaper
articles and editorials ranted about how the Polish immigrants
boosted crime. Next came claims of exploitation of Polish workers. Irish groups assigned alcohol and drug abuse to this immigrant group. In 2006, members of a far right neo-Nazi movement in Northern Ireland allegedly attacked Polish immigrants
on the streets or in their homes. Graffiti in Derry shouted "Poles
Out" underlined by a swastika.

"I know it's not my country, but it's my Europe . . . . We will defend ourselves. We are not slaves," said Radoslaw Sawicki in a 2005 interview, when he organized Poles working for the super-market chain Tesco warehouse in Dublin. The Irish trade union SIPTU supported him and his fellow Poles who were making about two hundred euros less a week than their Irish counterparts.

These articles resonated with what I knew of the Polish immigrants who populated the Ohio River Valley. Coalminers, mechanics and farmers, the Poles showed a strong affinity for unions, for solidarity and for their religion.

Sister Eily Deasy, recently retired teacher of the order Sisters of St. Joseph of the Sacred Heart, visited us on our tour and described the Polish Ella, the young woman who cared for her newborn niece. Sister Eily's sibling, Annette, recounted the devotion to the Church that Ella had shown, a trait inspiring trust from Annette and family.

"We don't mind them usually, but they are lowering the wages here. They work for less than we would," said a tour bus driver in Cork City when asked about the influx of Polish workers. That's one opinion shared by several press stories. Much of the wage depression though emanates from unscrupu-lous Irish and Polish companies that prey on unsuspecting new arrivals, offering low wages and claiming them to be on par with those of Irish workers, an unfortunate behavior of corpo-rations worldwide.

"I think the immigration is fine. We're getting used to it," opined the perky, red-haired proprietress of an Irish goods shop in the upscale tourist haven of Kinsale, County Cork.

"But I worry we'll lose who we are, what makes us Irish. You can go up through Ireland and not meet an Irish person in the restaurants and shops," she continued, straightening the hats and fabric bags on display.

At a Kinsale bookstore, the blonde twenty-something clerk with the pink chiffon scarf tied jauntily around her neck and seated at the register offered another view.

"I think the immigration is great. We like to have new people in. The Irish have had to endure so much criticism and prejudice over the years about themselves, I would hope we won't do that to others arriving here."

Ireland has traditionally dealt head-on with certain immigration issues. When some immigrant factions to England crossed the Irish Sea to birth their offspring in Ireland for citizenship, the government changed the law. They decreed that a person must live or work in the country two to three years before their child can become an Irish citizen at birth.

The Irish have always dealt with many of their challenges through music. Like the Irish, I turned to music for answers as well. Like a bee to pollen, I move toward it. I can hear an accordion a mile away. On any recording, my ear tunes in to the melodious chords from every squeezebox. My mother, in her sainted wisdom, proclaimed there would be at least one musician in our family, and that would be me. I learned to play a proper Polish polka beginning at age five.

One night at the Armada pub in Kinsale, County Cork, Sean Pol and accordion joined a group of four other musicians. In the daylight hours, he said he labored as a validation engineer two miles down the road at Eli Lilly. With an infectious smile and his instrument strapped to his chest, Sean Pol smoked Irish jigs on his American-made John Allan Hohner. The rhythm and tone sent me back to the ritual Saturday nights of Polish weddings at home and the all-day Sunday Polka Party on our fifties black radio.

As the four musicians cranked out the flings and jigs, I could see Frankie Fudale and sons, Billy and Jimmy, and their orchestra busting out polkas and mazurkas as the townspeople back in Maynard, Ohio, danced well into the Sabbath. Whiskey and beer flowed freely.

The Irish pub scene, with professional and amateur musicians wandering or invited in, also brought back scenes of many a family party with cousins brandishing their instruments and Uncle Joe huffing on his harmonica. I was always commanded to break out the black and ivory accordion to play those darn polkas, including *Mila Baba Koguta (A Lady Had a Rooster)*—my mother's favorite.

In addition to a love for lively music, Poles share the Roman Catholic religion with the Irish. While some resurgence in paganism and spirituality imbues the island, Ireland remains a Catholic country. With younger generations stoked by the Celtic Tiger's manna-first focus, travel and intercourse with same-aged populations on other continents, the Catholic Church's influence has waned. Yet the 2006 Irish Census found that 3.68 million Irish of the country's 4.6 million inhabitants check the Catholic box for religion.

The Catholic Church in Ireland now has fervent new supporters. Away from home, Poles continue their fervent attendance and devotion to the mass. At St. Augustine's Catholic Church in Cork City, long lines of Polish young men wend around the pews as each waits his turn for the confessional on a Saturday evening. Father Pat Moran, pastor at St. Augustine's for thirty-seven years, is elated at the energy contributed by the Polish congregants. The weekly Polish mass runs for ninety minutes, drawing some Irish locals among a capacity crowd. Some Irish parishioners view the Poles as Irish in the 1960s, when they dispersed throughout the world like so many dandelion seeds because of the economic condition at home.

Michael O'Brien, our regular taxi driver in Crosshaven, County Cork, spoke strongly on the topic of Polish immigration.

"I'm happy about it," he said. And well Michael O'Brien should be, since he married Marianne, who crossed over from Poland ten years earlier. Michael said he hired Marianne for a job at his taxi employer. And the rest is history.

"She cooks Polish food for me, and some Irish dishes as well," said Michael proudly. Recently Michael and Marianne O'Brien became new parents of a bonny lass, six-month-old Michelle, named after her papa.

"When I came to Crosshaven two years ago, only six Poles lived here. Today there are over one hundred Polish," said Magda, the dark-eyed energetic waitress at the Anchorage pub in Crosshaven. Magda had followed her accountant husband to Ireland, bringing their two young sons, aged three-and-a-half and two years.

"In Poland the minimum wage is two hundred euros a month. Here in Ireland, I can make two hundred euros for three days of work at this pub," explained Magda with a bright smile. In Crosshaven, her family finds it easy to blend in, noting that they have Irish, French, Spanish and German friends.

"I work here as a break from my sons," she cheerily confessed, turning her energy to delivering the best bowl of seafood chowder of our Ireland stay. Later, Magda noted that the forty years of Communism had created much infighting and distrust of government in Poland so that many "half hate, half love" Poland. She plans to enroll her boys in an Irish school, stay ten years, and see what happens back home.

Ireland has surprised itself, it seems. The new influx of immigrants resonates with so many Irish. For generations, they left their island in search of work. Not always welcome in foreign lands, today's Irish try to do one better.

During my stay, O'Brien Press announced they were translating the popular guide *How the Irish Live* into . . . Polish, of course. According to the news announcer, "This is a new group sharing our island with us and let's give them the traditional Irish welcome—*Céad Míle Fáilte*, One Million Welcomes."

The Irish have some lessons for us all on immigration and graciousness. Their openness of spirit provides a glimpse into the modern Irish soul. Indeed, 'tis much like the Irish soul of old. So much so, it makes a person feel liking stomping and twirling. Ah yes, strike up that Irish polka and let's all dance!

LE COEUR DE CORK

LENNY KARPMAN

rian holds court on a rectangular stone slab throne on Patrick St. in Cork's City Center. I ask him for directions to the English Market. "Are you wanting to have some lunch there or to look into the heart of Cork?" He places his right fist over his left chest and heart. My notepad and camera have given me away. I place my fist, as well, over my heart and answer, "Lub dub." As a food writer, I always go to markets first. I hope that this market will be my window into the very essence, the heart of Cork, its customs, history, culture, especially its people. His words resonate. Maybe I'll find lunch as well, while searching for only-in-Cork comestibles. Perhaps I'll also find in "New Cork" a microcosm of the new Ireland.

He flashes me a smile twice as wide as mine, but with half the teeth. A breeze catches his scraggly white hair. It stands up like a dandelion puff. His cheeks are purple, nose bulbous, and chin so small it looks like an upper Adam's apple. He directs me to the back entrance off an alley. "*Slán*," he says. "Go in good health."

As I cross the threshold into the market, I am awestruck by this architecturally stunning modern antique. Inside the grand hall, red, yellow, green and gold colors shine in light that diffuses through the leaded glass ceiling, not at all how I envision a 1788 vintage market. It is pristine and odorless except for wafting fragrances near the flower stand. It is nothing like the original Babel of wagons and carts under canvas, reputedly smelling from dead flesh and rotting produce. I was deceived by the alleyway leading to the entrance. It is gloomy, gray, dirty and old. The market arches have alternating black and white capstones radiating above hoary brick like a mosque in Southern Spain.

I walk to a relic waterless fountain, oxidized blue-gray with age in the center of the hall and turn a slow three-sixty with my eyes feasting in every direction. "Excuse me, Sister," I say as my dervish movements propel me into one of three Catholic nuns in gray habit, taking long purposeful strides across the concourse.

In the distant past, the market was exclusively Protestant. No Catholic merchants, customers, and surely no nuns were allowed. The market sat in the midst of affluent Protestant homes on an island in the Lee River. Gates on the two bridges were locked at night, the Irish market for Catholics residing outside the gates. The island market was therefore called English. The wealthy clientele bought offal, organ meats from cows, pigs and sheep, to feed their servants and pets. Today there are no gates on the bridges. People of all sizes, colors, religions and ethnicities flow around me as one.

A fellow browser sees the collision. Patrick, as old as Brian, shorter and round as a turnip, chuckles "You were run into by the Church, were you? You got to look out for all of them these days. Everyone is in such a hurry. Not me and Peetey. We need to watch where we lean or sit, out of the way of them. This here is Peetey. We sailed together when we were lads." Peetey is skinny and stooped, barely five feet tall, wrinkled as a prune, and has nicotine-yellow fingers. The market is smoke-free. They both are wearing tattered navy-blue jackets. Patrick's has buttons. Patrick tells me about the fire in the eighties and how they saved the fountain, reused the timbers and recast the wrought iron stanchions and filigree. An influx of local artisans, a balcony restaurant, and imported foods caused the site to evolve even further. But, to my eyes, the predominant change has been the arrival of new residents from Poland, Lithuania, Nigeria, China, Japan.

Patrick points down the aisle to the left. "Be sure and try some of our new Cork cheese down the way." Peetey flips a forty-year-old Zippo lighter over and over between his fingers like a gambler with a poker chip. It's the signal. Peetey needs to go outside for a smoke. They shake my hand with gusto, smile their asymmetric smiles, and amble slowly toward the Spanish arches.

Dutifully, I head for the cheese. There used to be only a single cheese-seller and he had just one cheese, a large round of

Emmenthaler. It was so expensive that buyers were few. As a result, the end cut was always dry and hard. It was part of the purchase.

A knowledgeable young man named Tim offers me local cheese wisdom and tastes. I purchase several small pieces. Of two dozen local cheeses, these are my favorites:

Carrigaline—smoked or herb & garlic rounds,

Cashel Blue—milder and less salty than European blues,

Durrus—an award winning delicate farmers' cheese made from raw cow's milk (not recommended for first trimester expectant mothers),

Local Vintage Cheddar—bargain rectangles,

Gubeen—cow's milk rind cheese with flavor akin to French Rebochon and

Killian Brie—silky soft and runny with no hint of the sour over-ripe flavor that accompanies French cheeses, aged excessively to reach comparable texture.

I speculate aloud that a nice spicy *kielbasa* might go well with the last of my small cheese purchases. Another shopper, Waclav, who moved to Cork from Krakow, overhears my mumbling. "The *kielbasa* here is too much fat and garlic. Try Czech spicy." After English, Polish is the second most common language these days. Adjacent to the cheeses at On the Pig's Back, lean and lovely young Maria is grilling sausages. "I can have one ready for you in five minutes if you like."

I like. She dresses it with sweet red relish. Waclav is right. It is great, balanced flavor and enough bite to warm my lips.

Maria smiles with justified pride.

Under the arch, I sit with my sausage and a strong cup of coffee. Cork's new gentry parade past. Table mate Irene, with blue tinted white page-boy from another generation, is as chatty and friendly as Brian and Patrick. She tells me that these days housewives, babes in tow, have gone to the suburbs and their supermarkets. "They used to stop by Kay O'Connell's for a piece of battleboard, mackerel, or herring and a bit of the gossip. They won't get better value or variety than here," she says emphatically. She enumerates—and I record—all the types of food that are unique to Cork.

Battleboard is salted ling cod, once a staple, now a rarity. I head for Kay's, but Kay is gone. Her sons run the place now, pleasant, efficient, modern businessmen, moving politely but quickly among the customers, far too busy to swap gossip. They sell lobster, oysters, mussels, monk fish, razor clams, plaice, hake, salmon, black cod and a little battleboard tucked in a corner.

I notice an Asian woman, artfully made up, who wears a crimson and gold scarf that shines like a beacon among the ubiquitous brown, black, gray and navy native garb.

As I arrive at the vegetable stand, an old woman clad in long black coat and gray scarf walks up beside me. "Hello Mary," the clerk, Judy, sings out. Mary can't hear very well. Her worn purse, sensible shoes and weathered shopping bag are black. Surrounded by fruits from North Africa and the Caribbean, Mary eyes only local apples. Puzzled, she inspects a row of designer lettuces. Judy answers a tinny rendition of Handel's Messiah on her cell phone and turns away. Mary points to a small purple head of radicchio and asks me if it's cabbage. "It's a kind of bitter lettuce," I answer. She chooses butter lettuce, two carrots, a small head of spring cabbage and four potatoes, the same choices that she has made "for fifty years," Judy whispers, off the phone. She says so many old folks are rigid culinary traditionalists, just like Mary.

Atop Irene's only-in-Cork food list is drisheen, sheep's blood pudding made with an herb called tansy. I've never heard of tansy. Neither has Judy. She points across at a butcher who sells drisheen and might know about tansy.

Undaunted, I head there. Drisheen, he tells me, is lighter in color than black pig's blood pudding, a mixture of sheep and cow blood, seasoned with the mystery herb. It is packed into tubes of inverted sheep intestine, boiled, split open, sliced into rounds, and usually added to sweet and fork-tender tripe, sim-mered in milk with onions for hours. He is shy and asks to remain anonymous. Barely forty, far too young to know these tales first hand, he regales me with old market stories for an hour, mostly about the times when there were several drisheen makers. Now there is one. His heart is with tradition and his elders. In his meat case sit logs of local spiced beef, another Cork special on Irene's list. Brined in water and stout, the beef is rolled in a mélange of thirty-two spices. I ask which thirty-two. "I'd tell you if I knew them, but if I did, I'd be a million-aire." We sample and speculate together that among them are ginger, nutmeg, salt, cinnamon, allspice, white pepper and thyme. He tells me "Paul Murphy might know more of the spices, but he's left for the golf course." He shows me bodice and skirt. Bodice is pig's rib cage that has been cured and salted. Homemakers boil it. Skirt is diaphragm, simmered in brown sauce with kidneys, Cork's answer to steak and kidney pie. But I'm still looking for tansy. The shy butcher points me toward Mr. Bell's two oriental food stores with wide selections of herbs and imported products from Bulgaria, China, Greece, Japan, Korea, Poland, Turkey. Very impressive inventory. No tansy.

The clerk at Mr. Bell's suggests a visit to Tom, an award-winning butcher, another kindly and well-informed man. Though he has one offering from my list, curbeen, or boiled pigs feet, he can't enlighten me on tansy, and suggests visiting Patricia, the all-knowing queen of tripe at O'Reilly's next to the front door. She is as sweet and informal as a long lost friend. She hasn't tasted tansy, but she describes it as looking like wild thyme with yellow button flowers, in her neighbor's yard. Tansy mythology implies that it is good for arthritis and keeps away flies.

Three hours after the Czech sausage, my belly rumbles. One last list item before lunch, buttered eggs. The clerk at Moynihan's doesn't know much about them except they cost less than half a Euro more a dozen than ordinary eggs and only older folks buy them. He calls his boss, Thomas, out of the back room to explain. "It was the sailors," he smiles. "No refrigeration at sea and they didn't want rotten eggs.

Nowadays, people buy them for nostalgia." A thin coat of butter seals the pores. Airtight, the eggs stay "fresh" longer.

A few feet away, the stairway climbs to the Farmgate Café on the balcony overlooking the market. Time to try tripe, onions and drisheen. It's supposed to be a morning-after cure.

The hostess seats me at a cramped table for four in the crowd, across from two twenty-something women from Dublin smartly accessorized and next to an older woman dressed more formally, married to a local Corkonian. The Dubliners are sleeveless. The woman on my right has a lace hanky in her sleeve. They order upscale salads and diet coke. She, a scone and tea. The pair glance at their watches frequently and laugh nervously. She smiles patiently. Rachmaninoff plays over the din.

My tripe and drisheen comes. Tender and bland, drisheen has the consistency of softly scrambled eggs. I can't taste tansy, or any other herb, for that matter. Tansy, it seems, remains an ingredient because of tradition. Drisheen is neither foul nor memorable. The proper matron on my right pronounces "My husband loves it, but he loves all things unique to Cork." Across the table, the mod pair grimace.

Back outside, it starts to rain. Harried mothers with chubby kids race for McDonalds. I see Brian under an awning, talking with a young Rastafarian in rainbow colors. I wave. He raises his fist to his chest and calls out "Loob doob."

DONNAGHA WHITE

※

This town witnessed the wrong of a nation
in Donnagha White and his condemnation;
hit hat the hood of those judged to die,
a hangman's noose his collar and tie.

I've rushed all night with no rest or sleep,
lie a spring lamb lost in a flock of sheep,
with fear in my heart, mad fire in my head
to find my young brother already dead.

I mourned you first at the edge of the lake
and mourned you next at the gallows' stake,
I mourned again at the feet of your corpse
among the British and the British curse.

If I only had you among your own
in Ballinarobe or in Sligo town,
the scaffold they'd break, the rope they'd sever
and you'd walk home on your name and honour.

For no hangman's scaffold were you born,
but for reaping wheat and threshing corn,
for ploughing the top-soil left and right
and turning the red clay into sight.

Dead brother Donnagha, honest and true,
well I know those who betrayed you;
drinking and smoking and plotting all night
and stalking the dew at the day's first light.

You, Mulhall, who struck this blow
my brother was no thieving cow,
but an honest man in thin and in thick
who could knock a sweet tune from a hurling stick.

But Donnagha White, since the only truth
is the grandeur and grace of buckets and boots,
we'll lay you out in fine homespun
and send you off like a noble's son.

Desmond O'Grady ❀ Donnagha White

Mulhall, your sons were never united
and your daughters with dowries were never delighted!
our table's swept bare, the white boards full
with my brother, dead from a hang-rope's pull.

I see Donnagha's dowry coming home
and it is not cattle nor crops of his own
but tobacco and pipes and the long candles' light
and no boast brightens our boy's black night.

—DESMOND O'GRADY

Remember Us

CONNIE BURKE

Abandon all hope who enter here,
Out of this there is no redemption,
Whoever wrote this, he wrote it well,
For the same is written, on the gates of Hell.

The writing on the walls tells it all: the names, addresses, sketches and poetry the prisoners painstakingly scraped onto the cracked inner walls of the old Cork City Gaol, at different times called Sunday's Well or the Women's Gaol. The inmates tell stories of patriotism, courage, hardship and suffering that embrace the turbulent history of nineteenth and early twentieth century Ireland.

The enormous castle-like stone structure of Cork City Gaol lurks high above the city of Cork in the old-world leafy suburb of Sunday's Well (named for an ancient healing spring). From the arrival of the first prisoners in 1824 to the closing of its vermin-infested cells in 1923, every facet of the human condition is reflected in the writings on the walls and in the letters written by the prisoners.

Wouldn't I like to catch them,
How them I would squeeze,
I would kill them all with a number nine,
Those bugs and lice and fleas.

The Cork City Gaol experience is a grim reminder of an eerie, foreboding past. Life-like models of ill-fated inmates wait for you to enter their cold, damp, bug-ridden world. Many of the early prisoners were locked up for petty crimes such as stealing clothing, bread, domestic trinkets, sometimes a sheep. Snatching a loaf of bread could mean several months of imprisonment. Yet some starving victims of the Great Famine took advantage of the harshness of the law and deliberately stole small items so they might be incarcerated and receive a measure of food and shelter.

The Great Famine struck Ireland in 1845. The cause of the famine was a fungus which caused potato plants to rot in the ground, giving off an appalling stench. The majority of islanders were wretchedly poor, eking out an uncertain living on tiny plots of land farming potatoes and the crop failure proved fatal. More than half the island's crop failed. During the five years the Great Famine lasted one million people died. Many chose emigration over starvation, others intentionally committed petty crimes, thus choosing gaol.

"You lost your freedom, of course, but you were relatively warm, dry, and fed," explained Elizabeth Kearns, administrator of the Gaol Heritage Centre. "The early nineteenth century was not a good time to be poor."

Being poor was equated with being guilty. Nine-year-old Edward O'Brien was jailed for three weeks for stealing two brass ball cocks. With both of his hands tied to a fixture on the cell wall, his bare back was whipped twice weekly for the three weeks he was in prison. The fixture on the wall, like the poetry, remains.

Cell after cell, we meet the inmates and read the writing on the walls. Sitting in a chair nursing her new-born son in the western wing is Mary-Ann Twohig. She was barely sixteen years old and pregnant when she stole a cap in hopes of selling it to get money for food. Her baby boy was born in prison. Her sentence was reduced to two months after her baby became ill.

But nursing her child did not exempt her from the hardship prisoners endured while incarcerated. The summer timetable reveals that the bells woke the prisoners up at a quarter to six every morning. The Irish at the time wouldn't consider getting up before eight o'clock. But the prisoners were up and cleaning their cells before their half hour exercise regiment—a circular walk in the prison yard.

"Before the Celtic Tiger came to Ireland in the last decade, getting up early meant about eight o'clock. Very early was half past seven," said Elizabeth Kearns shaking her head. "But today everybody's up at a quarter to six. And they are sitting in traffic most of the time."

All prisoners were subjected to punitive labor. Men would work the treadwheels (used to grind corn for prison use), break stone, crank machines, clean the prison yards and cells, or paint. Less strenuous activities for men included weaving, shoe-making, tin work, tailoring, pegmaking, or picking oakum. Punitive labor for women included washing, cleaning and scrubbing the yards and cells, carding, spinning, sewing, making and repairing prison clothes and picking oakum. All the clothing and sheets (not blankets) were manufactured in the prison.

As the prison grew overcrowded, prisoners were deported from Ireland. Crowded into huge rough wagons known as tumbrels, they were taken down to Queenstown (now Cobh) and herded onto convict ships. At first most ships leaving Ireland only sailed in the summer months when the weather conditions were more favorable. But the sheer volume of emigrants as well as convicts forced ships to sail all year round despite threats of storms and icebergs. Though convict ships were also called "coffin ships," most offenders preferred being sent away from their homeland to enduring the squalor of life in the Cork City Gaol.

Oh what a pretty home we have,
You should call in and see
You'd always find us happy,

Myself and the other three.
There's no glass in the window,
A blanket for the door,
A wooden bed to lie on,
And we are eating on the floor.

In the 1860s, many of the political prisoners were transported to convict ships. Among the infamous was John Sarsfield Casey, convicted at the age of nineteen for treason and transported along with sixty-two other Fenians to Western Australia. The Fenian movement had members in Ireland and elsewhere, primarily America and England. They had one simple desire for Ireland—independence from British rule. Some believed that the government in London, to solve the "Irish Problem," had deliberately done as little as possible to aid the people of Ireland during the Great Famine—a form of genocide—and concluded that the only hope for Ireland was a complete separation from Great Britain. If London was unwilling to grant this, then the Fenians would fight for it.

John Sarsfield Casey was pardoned in Australia and was one of the lucky ones who made it back to Ireland. Upon his return, he was noted for his work on behalf of the tenants of the Galtee countryside. He was carefully watched by the police as he wrote under the nom de plume, "The Galtee Boy" in the Fenian newspaper.

We want no hospitality,
We want no sympathy,
All we ask and long for,
Is our liberty.

A sadder tale is that of Brian Dillon. Growing up he was in a serious accident which resulted in curvature of the spine, and suffered from ill health thereafter. He attended the School of Art and became quite accomplished with brush and pencil. In 1865, Dillon was arrested for treason because of his association with the Fenian movement. The police, on searching his home in Dillon's Cross, found a pair of field glasses, some drawings, and incriminating letters sewn into the mattress of his bed. A guilty verdict sentenced him to penal servitude and the deep chill and sleepless nights in the Cork City Gaol made him seriously ill. A commission was set up to investigate the Fenian prisoners. Eventually, Dillon was transferred to a London jail for a few months before being set free. But by then, his health had deteriorated. His mother nursed him until his death barely a year after his release.

Sing robin redbreast, sing;
While listening to thy minstrelsy,
Through prison bars my soul will wing
To Ireland over the sea.

By the 1920s, many Republicans fighting in the War of Independence and the Civil War found themselves forcibly detained within the gaol's walls. Among the internees was the famous writer Frank O'Connor. Prominent novelist, short story writer, playwright and poet, he believed that as a member of the Irish Republican Army he represented his country in a justifiable way.

Other inmates included the infamous members of the *Cumann Na mBan*, the Irish republican women's paramilitary organization. Its constitution clearly dictated its purpose: "to advance the cause of Irish liberty" and "to teach its members first aid, drill, signaling and rifle practice in order to aid the men of Ireland." On Labor Day, the first of May, 1919, *Cumann Na mBan* members Kate Breen, Henrietta Woods, Bridget Glesson, Lizzie Foley and Margaret Cahill were collecting for the Prisoners' Dependent Fund without a permit. The following month police went to their homes and arrested them. They were brought to the barracks, tried and reprimanded for disturbing the peace. However, they ignored the courts instructions and were sent to gaol where they were warmly greeted by their Cork comrades.

They rose in dark and evil days,
To right their native land,
They kindled there a living blaze,
That nothing can withstand.
Alas that night can conquer right,
They fell and passed away,
But true men like you men,
Are plenty here today.

Perhaps the most illustrious internee involved in the struggle for Irish Independence was Countess Constance Markievicz. The daughter of a prominent Anglo-Irish family, she married a Polish nobleman and artist, Casimir Markievicz. She was the first woman elected to the British House of Commons but refused to take her seat in protest. Countess Markievicz was condemned to death for her part in the 1916 uprising but the sentence was commuted as women were not executed. Held in solitary confinement, she showed no resentment to her captors and spent her days reading, studying, painting and writing. She was released from prison after one year due to ill health and promptly returned to her republican activities with renewed vigor.

While grass[es] grow and waters run
There will be men to dare and die for Ireland.

The writing on the walls tells it all. From the days of the Great Famine to the foundation of the State, the Gaol's message continues. Well beyond the borders of Sunday's Well, across the Shaky Bridge and River Lee, we could still hear the voices of the inmates pleading,
"Remember us. We are a part of history too."

The Drummer's Heart

M.J. Pramik

The musicians whooped out a jig our first night at O'Donoghue's Pub, the epicenter of Irish music, on Dublin's Merrion Row. Cloistered in the front corner of the wood-paneled watering hole in the middle of the city, John Walsh organized his song list in his head. In the center of the musical ring, against the dusky wall sat José with a *bodhran* (bow rahn), the Irish open drum. José is not a very Irish name. José actually hailed from Spain. He said he just liked the sound of the instrument and had practiced enough to join in.

"Waltons factory, here in Dublin. You can find a good *bodhran* for 300 euros," José whispered to me as he passed by.

I'm sensitive to drums. Often the windows on my San Francisco home bulge and shake, not from earthquakes but from reverberations walloped out by my son Josef's practice on

101

his full drum kit and assorted tympanum. Base, two toms, snare and a radiant array of speckled cymbals. He practices on a flat rubber pad to "tighten his chops." Orange styrofoam earplugs securely in place, he extemporizes for hours with eyes semi-shut. To date, no police car has pulled into the drive nor has a neighbor reported the whole lot of shakin' that does go on.

One of Josef's mystified high school teachers once asked, "How can you stand his practicing?" She was definitely not a parent. My answer required only a second of reflection.

"But, it's music," I said matter of factly. And it is.

Josef's drumming has taken on a healing rhythm over the last several years. Mickey Hart, drummer for the Grateful Dead, offered that drumming heals the soul to a packed Grace Cathedral one Sunday in San Francisco. Josef sat in rapt attention in the front pew inhaling Hart's words.

When I travel, I am always alert to a new drum opportunity for Josef. On José's Dublin tip, I began to search for the perfect *bodhran*. Not the tourist contraption with stenciled Irish scene on the head, serving up dissolute sound. I had come to Ireland on a quest for the modern Irish soul. If I had not yet located that spiritual center, I had surely tripped onto the country's musical heart. In the fuchsia-laden countryside that is rural Ireland—County Cork—I began my search for the special *bodhran*, a birthday gift for Josef.

The open frame *bodhran* sets the heartbeat of Irish music. A large circle of wood, capped at one end by a smooth sheath of sheepskin, the drummer cradles the *bodhran* under his or her arm and hugs it tight against the body while sensually massaging the taught skin from the inside. With the other hand, the musician twiddles the double-headed beater or tipper against the outside surface.

A skilled *bodhran* player is a prized find for traditional Irish music groups. This frame drum is an exciting instrument in the right hands, layering a subtle sound to Irish folk music. To the untrained ear, the *bodhran* appears to be an easy path into a band and free pub ale. Not so, since the *bodhran* player works to match the tune and the melody.

One of Josef's music teachers explained it: "The drummer does not keep the rhythm. The drummer paints, he fills in the spaces of absence."

I had always thought otherwise: drummer equals beat.

"Not so, Mom," said Josef. "The bassist keeps the beat."

"Oh." Learn something new every day.

Church bells pealed eventide as we entered the Armada pub in Kinsale, County Cork. The chatter of the skittle aroused the crowd at the Armada. With that heavenly accent Irish barmaids have patented, the waitress with eyes the color of Ireland asked, "What can I get ya?" The fetid scent of the room bespoke many a spilled Irish whiskey.

As we settled into the bitterness of the night's first sip of stout, the musicians sitting at the center round table stoked their instruments. Balding and wiry, plumber Fenton Healy orgasmically twisted his body, caressing the *bodhran* while beating out the tune with either his hand or his baby-rattle-shaped tipper. Busker Ian MacLean, dreadlocks pulled back in a ponytail, plunked the banjo and biotech engineer Sean Pol o Taitin raked widespread fingers over his American-made John Allen accordion. Led by Diarmyid Grod, professional guitarist, they barreled through reel, jig, waltz and all music Irish throughout the evening. But of course, my eyes keyed in on Fenton who, sporting a pale mustache, cocked his head to and fro much like a rooster in the farmyard as he smacked the beat on his *bodhran*.

This starry night celebrated their first time playing all together, said accordionist Sean Pol. What good fortune for we pub patrons as the four young fellows spoke to our spirits. So inspired, I continued my search for that *bodhran* in earnest. After all, Josef was one quarter Irish by birth. A *bodhran* he should play.

Back at the B&B, I turned to the Internet. Why not find the *bodhran* online so I would not have to haul a suspect round shape through the nightmare security at Heathrow on my return? I thought that I could easily pick up a *bodhran* at the Waltons Musical Instrument Galleries on Frederick Street in Dublin and ship it to San Francisco to arrive in time for Josef's birthday. Brilliant. I flashed an e-mail to their web intake. Pascal Sallou of the Waltons Music Marketing Team zipped back a reply after his return from a long weekend:

"We don't really ship items to the U.S. as we have a distributor down there. I'd suggest that you contact them; they'll help you."—Pascal, Waltons Music Marketing Team, Waltons

Musical Instrument Galleries Ltd., Dublin.

I fired back, "I am a romantic. Buying the *bodhran* for my son's nineteenth birthday on the fifth of July in Dublin, Ireland, would be lovelier than a U.S. distributor. Thank you. Please, do you have a sixteen-inch tunable maple *bodhran*?" Pascal must have considered my frenzied request just another crazy American rant. He did not reply.

Several hamlets and taverns later, I happened on a magic circle of musicians at Buckley's pub in Crosshaven, Cork. The warm community oozed through the tight quarters. Buckley's smiling owner, Nina Casey, with her bob of short gray hair and crisp white- and black-striped shirt, served as high priestess, deftly delivering drinks to one and all.

The musicians that night at Buckley's underscored for me how my son could feel a well-loved part of a family when playing in such company. Several years after the breakup of our family, Josef had explained how he made it through the ensuing years in his one of his college essays:

"School became harder, family activities became scarce, and my life sometimes felt like everything was crashing down. This is when I turned to music to help me through this time. Jazz became my new dinner table as Art Blakey, Jackie McClean, and Josef Zawinul filled the plates, utensils, pots and pans . . . . All I want to do now is play music because it is what makes me happy. Writing music, playing music, even practicing, is

105

something I want to do. Once my parents separated, they each became busier and I had to find new ways to entertain myself, which music did so effortlessly and completely. Finding something I was passionate about taught me how to dig deeper in all of my studies."

I focused my listening at Buckley's. Jimmy, the *bodhran* player, also clacked two slender curved deer bones resembling spoons. Rhythmically twirling them like miniature batons with staccato wrist movement in midair, he created a spectacular percussive clucking sound.

"The bones are from his first wife," quipped a male patron with a wink at the next table. The proverbial Irish humor was in high cheer that night.

Jimmy's fellow musicians rounded out the evening with two gentlemen on shimmery guitars, Lucy (her dear parents beaming across the table from me) bowed a lively violin, a substantial young man jammed properly on a box accordion, and another fellow squeezed the *uilleann* pipes (*uilleann* for elbow) with his arm and elbow to amazing effect. At times a banjo would appear and join in. Then a random pub patron would burst into song, crooning a heart-rending version of "I Have Loved You Dearly." Mesmerized by the sheer force of the music, I came to understand Josef's belief that playing with other musicians indeed creates a family.

During a break in their music making, Jimmy answered my

questions about his *bodhran*, "Go to Cork and to the Living Tradition music store on McCurtain Street. It's across the street from Crowley's Music Shop."

The very next day, my last full day in County Cork, I made a beeline for the Living Tradition.

Locating the Living Tradition proved easy. Selecting the right *bodhran* did not.

Carl, the youthful shop attendant, began pulling out bodhrans. The shelves hosted at least fifty, or a hundred, of these wooden circles. Carl, a *bodhran* player himself, offered me his favorite.

"But this drum you like has no crosspiece in the back," I objected, neophyte *bodhran* observer as I was.

"I find the crosspiece limits my motion," said Carl. "I can move my hand all over the skin without it." He began to sound like Josef, who would get this point. He had me when it came to opinions on musical instruments.

While I stewed over the dozen or more *bodhrans* laid out on the carpeted floor, American-born Brian entered the shop. According to Carl, Brian was a premier *bodhran* player. Raised in Boston, he now lived in Cork with his mother, a local resident.

With his silver ear studs and black velvet jacket, Brian authenticated my choice of *bodhran*. Both young men took turns playing each drum considered. Their keen enthusiasm and glee recreated the joy I had seen in Josef's face for any drum. As they chatted about the quality of each drum played, I heard the deep sensual sound that Josef would find truly soulful. I had found that special *bodhran* with the unique sound.

"This is the *bodhran* I would want for myself," said Carl. I believed him. The sound was deep, subtle, resonant.

"Ay, a carnage of *bodhrans*," laughed Brian, smiling at all the drums randomly populating the shop floor. I offered to help put them away but the two young gentlemen would hear none of it.

"And which tipper do you want?" asked Carl. "Ya, you must have one of these," he said answering his own question. "Twenty-two euros for this exquisite thin stick of richly polished mahogany." He smiled as he lovingly wrapped it tightly in a thin sheet of paper.

Carting the eighteen-inch *bodhran* home through Heathrow security was my next task. With the aplomb of a spy, I managed to squish my backpack into the bodhran case without ripping the goatskin surface while carrying my laptop under my raincoat. At Heathrow, only one carry-on is allowed between planes that permit two carry-ons. I somehow managed to accomplish my goal. The Irish faeries must have been smiling.

My flight gently settled toward the gray-green waters of San Francisco Bay, with fog stretched over San Bruno Mountain and the Coast Range framing the western border of the peninsula. I cradled the *bodhran* in its black padded case. It was my son's nineteenth birthday. His sister and friend had prepared the evening's dinner for my son's starring role, even going so far as to bake and assemble his favorite chocolate-mint-chip ice cream cake.

"A drum, right, Mom? This is getting to be a habit. I can use it with my new compositions. Wait until you hear them."

He beamed his usual grin as he zipped open the black bag and stroked the taut surface of the *bodhran*. He immediately set the sound, the same one I had heard in Cork at the Living Tradition. I then noticed the twists and pulsations of his back muscles, akin to the movements of Fenton Healy in Kinsale and Jimmy at Buckley's in Crosshaven. While I had been busy with life, my son had truly become a drummer, a healer of the sadness that beats in all of us at times.

Ascending the stairs later that night, I caught sight of the *bodhran* in my son's bedroom, now a music studio. The *bodhran* nestled next to his snare, leaning against his Senegalese *djembe* and the Greek *dumbéleki*. In the hushed darkness of my return, these inanimate percussion instruments portrayed a family, all different, each with its own sound, joyful to be there, present with each other.

Mahler in Hi-B

Denise Altobello

mail from my husband Brian:

Thanks for the pictures. Didn't think they had "bars" in Ireland. Thought the Irish just had pubs. But if there was a bar around, I knew you'd be the one to find it.

How many miles from New Orleans did I travel? And where did I end up? In a bar. Listening to Billie Holiday. As usual.

My preparation for any trip is honed by years of teaching. Read. Take notes. Read some more. Research the "must see places" and "must do activities." Finally, organize the list: see churches; do bars.

In the city of Cork, however, the luck of the Irish fell upon me. This time, I didn't have to find the bar. The bar found me.

I must admit that my passion for such global bar-hopping is

at least in part an academic one. Teacher—and drinker—I'm also a groupie for my literary heroes: characters, writers and their settings. I've sipped Campari at the Danieli in Venice because Mark Twain did. I swirled absinthe in Paris because Arthur Rimbaud did. And most recently, I drank cheap red wine from a bladder in Pamplona because Lady Brett Ashley did.

With Ireland my destination in summer 2007, I was entering the land of the pub. My thirst for knowledge was piqued. First, I read *McCarthy's Bar*; then moved on to *A History of the Irish Pub*, followed by *The Parting Glass: A Toast to the Traditional Pubs of Ireland*. Once on the plane, I opened David Monagan's *Jaywalkin' with the Irish*, an account of his family's 1999 move to County Cork, and took special note of the Hi-B Bar, owned by the legendary Brian O'Donnell.

As expected, pubs abound in the Emerald Isle. I visited three from my list on my first Saturday evening in Dublin, yet in County Cork averaged only one pub a day. Sure, we visited the Spaniard Inn, a "must do" pub in Kinsale. And, yes, we enjoyed pub grub at another landmark, the Armada, where we delighted in the sometimes haunting, other times rollicking strains of a group of pony-tailed Irish musicians. The problem was carving out time for my own pub research.

One morning, after a tour of the city of Cork, our group crammed together at the bustling Farmgate Café overlooking the historic English Market. Over a lunch of icy raw oysters from the cold Irish waters, Donald Casey, a tall, elegant ninety-two-year-old pianist, took our requests and smiled as we sang

112

along to the predictable choices—"Danny Boy," the "Road to Tipperary" and even "When Irish Eyes Are Smiling." White-haired, and with what appeared to be a toupée on top, skirted in back by a giant comb-up instead of the more customary comb-over, he seemed the perfect accompaniment for our pints of Beamish, Guinness and Murphy's.

An old gent leaned over the piano top and sang along with us. Cheeks pink with the traditional Irish blush, he teased, charmed and basked in the attention of so many females. I lifted my glass as the man began distributing his business card: the words "Hi-B Bar" jumped at me. Could this be Brian—Monagan's most engaging and cantankerous character?

"Would you be Brian O'Donnell?" I asked.

"I would be he. And how do you know of *me*?" Puffed with pride, his tortoise-framed eyes narrowed their sights upon me. I refused to shrink under the magnified gaze of a man whose business card warned of a "talent to abuse."

"I read about you. Actually, you're on my A-list for Cork."

His laugh betrayed both his delight and his expectation that his bar and his name were so well known. He preened and joked a bit more with us before throwing down a farewell gauntlet to me. "I'm sure I'll see *you* soon."

Several hours later, I stood before the Hi-B's red awning flapping above a sign announcing the first floor's resident, Cork City Hair Extension and Wig Clinic. I climbed the dark staircase, opened the door and smiled. *I'm in.*

⚯

The Hi-B is cozy, with a fireplace in the corner flanked by patrons of all ages. Gold fleurs-de-lys adorn the faded red walls. The smell of beer and whiskey takes me home to a hundred such bars in my beloved New Orleans. Completing the perfect welcome for me is the voice of my idol, Billie Holiday, singing "My Man."

Sipping a Bushmills at the crowded bar, I hear, "Is this your first time at the Hi-B?"

I smile and nod, remembering the advice in *How to Down a Pint in a Real Irish Pub:*

"Eventually, one of the punters (bar patrons) will start a conversation . . . smile and nod—unless the person is frowning, in which case, frown and nod."

This punter is very definitely smiling. He introduces his friend, Michael, and says, "Everyone calls me 'Cookie.'" I tell them a bit about my Cork "A-list," and what I've read about Brian O'Donnell. Egged on by Guinness and me, they share even more stories. Each one begins with, "Remember . . .

—when Brian threw someone's cell phone into a beer when it rang?"

—when he drank Cookie's beer because Cookie had set his pint down on the wrong coaster and wasted a coaster?"

—the time he drank a man's beer who had the nerve to throw another log on the dying fire? The man protested, 'Hey, that's my beer!' Brian retorted, 'Hey, that was my wood!'"

—the patron who asked for a newspaper? Brian's retort: 'This is a bar, not a feckin' library! Get out!'"

Each tale ends with the same four word conclusion: "Brian is feckin' nuts!"

After a half hour or so of this banter, I ask, "Do you think I could take a picture? Of you two and of the bar?"

Michael hesitates. "You can take our picture, but we'd better do it outside. Brian might come in."

"Are cameras forbidden too?"

"Everythin' is when he has one of his fits on. He can be like the devil."

Cookie nods solemnly.

I smile and nod, "Right."

I place the photo-op on hold when I recognize one of the musicians from the previous night's pub-crawl. Pointing to the sign announcing live music on Wednesday nights, I nudge Cookie: "Today is Wednesday. Will he be playing?"

"Brian only likes classical and opera. In fact, if he comes in now, he'll probably turn off what's playing." Edith Piaf continues her "La Vie en Rose" despite the ominous threat.

Sipping a new Bushmills, I check out Brian's pencil sketches of famous patrons along the wall. Reputation for abusing customers aside, Brian is clearly a bit of a groupie. Like me. But I bet he wouldn't admit it.

Walking along the memento-studded wall, I note Brian's "A-list" of famous patrons:

Edward VII

Albert Einstein

Somerset Maugham

George Gershwin

Alexander Fleming

Jimmy Durante

Not such a classicist after all, is he? I giggle. *O'Donnell has range, judging from the equal billing he gives the discoverer of penicillin and Jimmy Durante!*

Another gentleman introduces himself with a wink and a smile and asks, "Would you be thinkin' of doing a story on Brian?"

"Maybe. I'm just poking about right now."

"Well, watch out, love. If Brian walks in, he'll hurl that notebook and you right out the place. He's feckin' nuts, you know."

Smile and nod, Denise. "Right." Where have I heard that before?

I sense Brian's entrance into the bar. Every pair of eyes in the place dart in his direction. Suspicion on his face, he marches behind the bar and peers about. He seems satisfied.

"Better hide that camera," Cookie warns.

Brian approaches the stereo. A push of a couple of controls, and the plaintive warbles of Paris's little sparrow fall silent. Immediately, the powerful strains of what I think are Wagner's fill the room. He spots me, smirks and waves an imaginary baton. "I see you found me."

"I found the bar, yes I have. My notes were right on target.

116

I even guessed that you would change the music to Wagner."

The imaginary baton freezes in mid-air. "So you think this is Wagner?"

"Isn't it?"

"Did you read my card?" his lips purse in exasperation.

"Yes."

"Where is it?" he demands.

I try to hand the card over.

Eyes magnified by both his huge glasses and his powerful indignation, he refuses. "Read it to me."

And there I see at the bottom of the card, under his name: "Well known Mahlerphile."

"Oops," I blurt. "I meant to say Mahler."

"So, you can read, can you? Listen. Close your eyes." Cookie and Michael laugh and shake their heads behind him. "This is the music of the gods. Here, take my baton. Feel the music."

A baton? Excellent. My own instrument of choice. A retired majorette with a resumé boasting Fancy Strut champion for four years straight, I'll dazzle him even with an invisible stick. On my second pass with the phantom baton, he grabs my hand, turns to my two supporters at the bar and says: "Feckin' Americans. Don't know anythin' about real music."

Undaunted, I admit, "I suppose you're right when it comes to classical music. I'm a bit more rhythm and blues, I'm afraid. But, I am *still* delighted to be here, Mr. O'Donnell."

"It's Brian." And with a completely unexpected twist in our conversation, he asks, "Are you this tall in bed?"

"Yep, pretty much," I laugh, pleased that my 5´4˝ stature has grown so impressive in the land of the wee people.

"I would never have talked to you in the café if I had known that you were this tall. What is your name?"

"Denise."

"Is that it? Denise?" Disapproval is palpable.

"Altobello. Denise Altobello."

"Are you Italian?"

Hmm . . . Are Italians favored for their contributions to opera? Or should I expect more points for my French and German roots? Wasn't Mahler German? I decide to hedge my bet. "No. I'm French and German. But my husband is Italian."

Like the professor tripping up an unsuspecting pupil, he barks, "So, you have a husband. Don't bring him here. What's his name?"

This time, I chuckle. "The same as yours. Brian."

"I wouldn't have talked to you if I had known you were married." He dismisses me with a turn toward the bar.

"Might I have a picture with you?" I persist.

"Why?"

I point to the wall of fame that circles the establishment. "I'm a bit like you, Mr. O'Donnell. I want to have a souvenir photo of the two of us together."

"I don't allow cameras in here."

"I'll be quick. I'll even stoop so that I look shorter in the picture."

"Who will take it?"

"Cookie will, I'll bet." I look over to the bar hopefully. Brian scowls but is clearly weakening.

I concede only slightly. "I'll turn off the flash so no one will even notice."

He steps in front of me and surrenders. "Okay. But the foreground is mine." *Works for me.* "And I'm not going to conduct for your silly picture."

"Agreed!" We shake to seal the deal.

"And you won't bring your husband here."

"Easy one," I assure him. "He's home in New Orleans. But he really would love this place."

"He's not welcome. But you are." He kisses my hand. "What do you do when you're not stalkin' old men in bars?" he poses.

"I'm a teacher."

"Then you'd best learn your Mahlers from your Wagners."

"Got it." I stoop for the camera.

Flash! *Damn!* I forgot to turn off the flash before I handed the camera to Cookie.

"Do they let *eejits* become teachers in America?" he thunders, invoking the Irish epithet for idiot.

"Not usually."

"Feckin' tourists," but his large eyes twinkle as he drops a kiss atop my head.

I knock back the rest of my whiskey, toasting my good luck that the Hi-B's notorious owner walked right out of the pages of my research and into my afternoon.

Sheela-na-gig

Laurie McAndish King

heela-na-gig's invitation is fraught with danger. Our relationship began with my quick peek at a wildly porno-
graphic image in Thomas Cahill's popular book, *How the Irish
Saved Civilization*. An ancient goddess, Sheela is rendered sym-
bolically, stripped of all but the essential features. She is naked,
bald, and breastless, and reaches both arms behind her bent
legs, using her hands to spread her genitals wide open—as wide
as a barn door—in exuberant invitation. There was no question
in my mind about the figure's intended meaning. As soon as I
saw her, I was transfixed.

Evolutionary biology is my calling; sex, transformation,
and renewal are my religion. I knew I would have no peace
until I found this wild and fearless female creatrix. But how
would I locate the figures? My guidebook didn't even mention

them. Could I go around asking civilized folks on the streets of County Cork where to find an ancient erotic goddess?

"Do you have an image of Sheela-na-gig?" I began at the Tourist Center in Kinsale, a charming seaside village known for its fine crafts, world-class cuisine and yachting activities. The buildings in Kinsale are well kept and brightly painted, and many are decorated with baskets spilling over with colorful flowers; they're accustomed to tourists here. "I see you have reproductions of old Celtic carvings."

Margaret, a young shopkeeper, regarded me curiously. "Gosh, I haven't thought about Sheela-na-gig since I was a wee girl. She was a screaming woman, wasn't she?" Margaret pantomimed holding her mouth wide open from both sides.

Hmmm. Right position, wrong orifice.

"When the monks came and brought Christianity, they didn't like her. That's all I really remember."

Was Margaret just being polite, or did she really believe that Sheela-na-gig was a screaming woman? Perhaps that was the way her genteel mother had described the goddess to a young and innocent girl. ("Yes, Maggie darling, she was screaming, and the monks didn't like her making all that racket. It was so unladylike.")

A second shopkeeper, twenty years older, stood nearby, shifting nervously from one foot to the other, and tittering with quiet embarrassment. "And what about you?" I asked, "Have you heard of Sheela-na-gig?" Surely she knew about a goddess who had been worshipped throughout the British Isles for centuries.

"Oh, no!" she sputtered hurriedly. "I'm English. I haven't heard of her a' tall!"

I asked around a bit more, buttonholing women in shops and on the street, but got nowhere. Either they had never heard of Sheela-na-gig, or they weren't admitting to it.

Clearly, a new approach was in order.

I determined to ask Sister Eily, a retired nun we were visiting with. Sister Eily had grown up in Ireland, and ran off when she was only sixteen—with her father's reluctant permission—to Australia to join the Order of St. Joseph of the Sacred Heart. Here was a fearless woman. After many years of service, Sister Eily had retired and returned home to Ireland. She wore street clothes, sensible shoes, and a white, furry vest she'd bought for fifteen euros in a thrift shop.

Indelicate though the question might be, I was certain Sister Eily would tell me the truth. After all, nuns—even retired ones—aren't allowed to lie. They are also tough as tires; the sister didn't even blink at my question, although the right side of her mouth did curl up in a small, sly smile. She replied with an Irish lilt, "Oh, very little is known about Sheela-na-gig."

I waited.

"She's the fertility goddess. A woman would go back into the church after giving birth to give thanks to Sheela-na-gig. She would go alone, or with a few female members of her clan, and go at a quiet time when no one else was there. My mother would have done this, with her mother and her sister. I always wondered, in my heart, why the father did not give thanks as well, since it was his child, too."

Sister Eily mused that giving thanks to a fertility goddess "isn't really part of the Christian tradition." She thought it had most likely been a holdover from pagan tradition, explaining that "pagans, like the rest of us, worship God the best way we know how."

I next inquired about Sheela at a pub, where a green-eyed waitress with tight jeans and an easy smile raised my hopes. "She's a fertility goddess," Irene said. "There are no fairy tales about Sheela-na-gig, and I'm not surprised that many people you've spoken with haven't heard of her. The old ways are being forgotten, aren't they? You'll find a site in Ballyvourney, on N25 past Macroom. Go out to a rural area, and ask the old men; they'll know."

I was surprised at Irene's suggestion that I ask a man about Sheela-na-gig, but the opportunity presented itself when I met Desmond O'Grady, one of Ireland's greatest living poets. And I couldn't resist.

Dr. O'Grady had not shaved that morning. His pale blue eyes were watery; his eloquent hands waxy. His hair was grey, wild and wiry. O'Grady wore a tattered red bandana around his neck; a wrinkled, sage green shirt; and crumpled, pale pink linen pants that looked as though they had been inadvertently washed with the bandana. He had been, long ago, a secretary to Ezra Pound and a good friend of Samuel Beckett.

During lunch, O'Grady revealed ambivalence toward the feminine, dispensing such wisdom as, "Women are only supposed to write checks," and "Cairo is a slum, except for the sphinx and her inviting orifice." His candor was promising; O'Grady was clearly no stranger to the earthier side of life. What did he think of Sheela-na-gig? I had to ask the question that was constantly on my mind, if not my lips.

O'Grady knew her, all right. He looked me straight in the eye and warned, "Stay away from Sheela-na-gig; she's good for nothin' but trouble! She'll take you for everything you've got, and then she'll come back for more." Then he ordered salmon and chips and a Beamish, admonishing the waiter not to forget the chips.

"Have you ever actually met Sheela-na-gig?" one of our party asked.

"Oh, yes!" the great poet whispered. "'O'Grady,' she said, 'I'm tough, and I live on Tough Alley. The farther down you go, the tougher it gets, and I live at the last house.'"

But the last house on Tough Alley is not Sheela's only abode. She was once prominently positioned in medieval churches and castles throughout Ireland and beyond, even onto the Continent. From Kirkwall Cathedral in the Orkney Islands to Tracton Abbey in the south of Ireland, from Killinaboy Church in the west to Royston Cave in the east, Sheela's image spread widely across the British Isles. In Dunnaman, Cavan, and Killua, prominent rib bones give her a skeletal appearance; the Brigit's Well figure at Castlemagner and the Crofton-on-Tees image look oddly like current depictions of space aliens. In Caherelly, Sheela's vagina is as large as her breasts, and in

Oaksey and Kilsarkan it is bigger than her head! Often Sheela's face is moronic; sometimes it is frightening. At times there is no face at all. But the Sheela-na-gig figures have one thing in common: an invitation to the great and fertile darkness.

Especially in Ireland, which was slow to adopt Roman Catholicism, ancient pagan imagery was commonly incorporated into early Christian iconography. For example, the Ballyvourney figure, which sits above a window in St. Gobnait's Church, was regarded as an image of St. Gobnait, who was the same person as St. Brigit, who was a personification of the pre-Christian Brigit, goddess of light and literature. Since the Reformation, most of the Sheela figures have been lost, destroyed, or disfigured; those that remain are often hidden in out-of-the-way corners. But they can still be found, and I was determined to do so.

I asked Benny, our knowledgeable guide, whether there were any Sheela images in County Cork. Guides here, as in much of the rest of the world, have an extensive understanding and recall of history and folklore, and are required to pass lengthy, exhaustive exams before being licensed. Surely Benny would know.

"Yes," he responded slowly, and after some consideration. "I'm sure I've seen a Sheela image nearby, right over a doorway . . . but I cannot remember where. Maybe you should check the museum."

Stella Cherry, a lean scholar with a dry sense of humor, is curator at the Cork Public Museum, and kindly consented to show me the two Sheela-na-gig figures in the museum's collection. They were not on public display. "The Irish don't seem to care about the figures," Stella explained, "But Americans are crazy for them." Stella had written a monograph about Sheela-na-gig in order to provide more information for the Sheela-seekers who besieged her with questions. She even fielded a visit from "an American Professor of Vaginal Imagery," visiting Ireland to do some post-graduate research.

Writing up the information presumably allowed Stella to send searchers—and researchers—off to view the figures *in situ*, rather than spending her already-busy days communing with Sheelas in storage. Stella handed me a copy of her article, *Sheela-na-gigs from County Cork*, published in the Journal of the Cork Historical and Archaeological Society, and led me to a closet that housed a fuse box, a washbasin, multiple mops and brooms, cleaning supplies . . . and, on the floor, two Sheela-na-gigs. Stella left me alone with them.

Each figure is a *bas relief* about two feet long, and is depicted standing upright, with fairly straight legs. Both have straight left arms, and right arms that are slightly bent at the elbow. Neither figure has ears, hair, breasts, or rib bones.

The carving known as the Tracton Abbey Sheela is in white stone and has a heart-shaped head with large, deep-set eyes, a small nose, tiny mouth, and narrow chin. The arms and hands do not touch or overlap the body. A deep indentation in the center of the figure, in stark and insistent contrast to the rest of the convex surface, represents the genitals. It is frightening.

The Ringaskiddy figure is carved in what appears to be golden sandstone. It has a large bald head with narrow-set eyes, a long nose and a wide mouth. A long, slender torso leads to short legs in a pigeon-toed stance. The figure's hands rest aside its genitals, which are represented with a simple, prominent, vertical line. Ringaskiddy aroused in me a feeling of amused affection.

I admit, though, I was disappointed. The features were more difficult to discern than I had expected, and these two both lacked the explicit, manual reference to genitalia that most Sheelas include. In fact, Stella refers to the figures as "wannabe Sheelas," since "there is no real attempt to bend the legs." Even so, I felt fortunate to be able to spend some time with them.

Scholars disagree about Sheela's significance. Some say she was believed to have the power to "turn the evil eye" and ward off enemy attacks, and for this reason was often placed on castle walls. Others suggest she was the Roman Catholic Church's way of communicating the evils of lust to a largely illiterate congregation, explaining her frequent residence in the remains of medieval churches. Still others insist she was a fertility goddess, beseeched by new brides and barren wives, prayed to by midwives and laboring women, and profusely thanked by blessed new mothers.

These explanations seem wanting. Surely the "good luck" idea is overly simplistic. As for the second option, Sheela is not attractive; rather, she is often frightening. She certainly represents something other than comely sexuality. And the fact that

Sheela's breasts and buttocks are not emphasized—in fact, her breasts are usually missing entirely—differentiates Sheela-na-gig from fertility figures. (Contrasting, for example, with the voluptuous pre-Columbian fertility goddesses.)

I prefer a fourth explanation: Sheela-na-gig, like the Indian goddess Kali, represents the devouring mother archetype—the source of life, death, and regeneration. She is "womb as tomb," the Great Mother whose capacity for destruction is requisite for the creation of new life. And her invitation, both terrifying and liberating, is nothing less than an opportunity to experience emotional death, transformation and rebirth.

No wonder the images have been disfigured, hidden and destroyed. They represent the feminine as the source of life, challenging the patriarchal father-as-creator perspective. Further, their symbolism embodies the unity of life and death, incorporating the "shadow" as essential to wholeness, rather than an evil to be overcome, or, at best, repressed. Little wonder, too, that the Sheela figures have attracted so many brave and crazy New-Age seekers, whose souls cannot bear the dissociative split of light from dark, and who ache for the powerful transformative process that is the Great Goddess's promise.

As for me, I've found a touchstone, a vivid reminder of my own connectedness to the circle of life and death. And I'll be a regular visitor at the last house on Tough Alley.

The Nuns, the Stones and the Spirits

Joanna Biggar

     t was hard to know what to expect from touring Ireland with a nun whom I'd first met on my deck overlooking San Francisco Bay while downing margaritas together. But I did know this: Sister Eily, with her fine-boned, elfin face, saucy red hair, her lithe body and spirit, and her easy laugh was good fun—good *craic*—as I learned to say in Ireland.

What I would find in my travels with her was what I came to think of as the essence of Ireland: great wit and delight rooted in a deep sense of the spiritual, derived in equal measure from beauty and from sorrow.

Eily had arrived on my deck that spring day in 2004 for a little end-of-year staff party for my colleagues at St. Martin de Porres Middle School in the inner-city neighborhood of West Oakland, California. Sister Teresa, Eily's younger sister and the school's religion teacher, was and is one of my best friends. With her great heart, warmth, good Irish backbone, and of course her West Cork accent tempered by several years in Georgia, she is beloved by everyone. I've especially treasured those moments when West Cork meets West Oakland: such as when our whole student body recites the Irish Blessing in Gaelic; or when Teresa is called upon to resolve some dispute and responds, "Aye, then, we'll *sert* (sort) it all out," to which some bewildered child inevitably looks at me and shrugs, "What she be sayin'?"

So when Eily, en route back to Ireland after forty years' teaching in Australia, passed by our little community, all were charmed by her, too—and her Cork accent flavored with Australia. At the time of our party, in the company of three Irish nuns all enjoying "a wee dram" (pitchers) of margaritas, I did not imagine that a few years hence I'd meet Eily again with a group of travel writers on her home turf.

Beforehand, in the many exchanges she sent by email from her apartment in Dublin, where she now lives with another, elderly, nun, she told me that she would particularly like to share with me and others her experiences at Dromberg in West Cork, and at spectacular Newgrange, in the Boyne Valley, both Neolithic religious monuments fashioned from stone. Hence she joined us all on an all-day bus trip through West Cork that included Dromberg. She was fresh from a retreat filled with lectures, prayers, meditation—and fun. "Every night," she said, "at the end of the day, we'd put on the tapes and do the Irish dances."

As the bus drove deeper into the countryside of West Cork, the land, though green and lovely, grew poorer—a fact well-known to the Catholic Irish who were consistently pushed to the rock-scrabble hard places by English overlords and the dominant Protestants. When we passed close by the poor, hilly farm country that had been home to Eily and Teresa, I remembered a remark Teresa had once made to a class of students: "When I was your age, I had never seen a black person—nor a Protestant, for that matter." At the time I had been puzzled, but now I understood. In this land beyond the Pale, there were no Protestants, let alone non-Irish races.

Then on the bus, Eily added her own musings, "I thought as a child that if you ever saw a Protestant church and looked through the window, it was a sin. But it will all come round again, and hopefully we will all be one." As for religion itself, she added, "you know at heart all religions are the same."

What I came to understand she meant was not just a reconciliation of Catholics and Protestants, but of all religions and our connection to our own pagan pasts. "I think paganism is cultural," she said speaking of her own Celtic heritage. "We have so many holy wells, streams, stones, the water and the moon. The circle in the Celtic cross is more than the sun, but the whole of creation."

Arriving at Drombeg, I walked with Eily along the short path to the circle of seventeen standing stones erected two-and-a-half millennia ago. The site on a small ridge was set in a patchwork of green, with a gray mist and a taste of the sea close by. The grass was a-litter with wildflowers, yellow daisies. This place held the ache of Ireland, its beauty. Filled with layers of wonder, I tried to imagine the ancient nomads who worshipped the sun here, the way they cooked, as evidenced from the pottery and hearths uncovered, and how they buried their dead. I wondered at the identity of the youth whose bones had been found buried in the monument's center. A human sacrifice?

Standing in the center of that circle representing the sun, I closed my eyes to hear again in my head Eily's story of why, after all those years, she had returned from Australia for good. "I went to bits after my mother's death," she told me. At that time she had come to nearby Drombeg to feel peace as she stood alone in the circle, trying to cast off the burdens of grief. "I got strength from the stones in Australia, but part of my soul wouldn't connect with those stones. I believe the minerals and soil in the place where we are born are in us. Sometimes I walk on these mounds and feel all the sadness."

She also knows she is not alone in that connection with her native stones. Despite centuries of trying to destroy "paganism" on the part of the Church, it thrives, as the droves who still visit Drombeg bear witness. They come to leave offerings of oranges, flowers, shells, and to honor the solstices, the moon, sun and stars. "It's the young people who come here," Eily explained. "The Catholic Church had a great hold on the people, and that's gone, or lessened, which isn't a bad thing. But it's the young who will rediscover in their own way." As for her own way, her acceptance of the sacred nature of her native place and her beliefs as a Catholic nun, she put it like this: "The people who came here belonged to the circle of God, and then Jesus came down to explain who that God is. They saw God through His creativity."

⊗

As my borrowed Irish luck would have it, after our journey together in Cork, I got to visit Sister Eily again. On the train back to Dublin, I anticipated seeing her with growing delight. I loved her stories, all told in that lilt in which "no" rhymes with "shoe," even if many were sad. She told me of the mournfulness she had experienced when walking hilly lanes in West Cork not knowing she was treading mass graves of those who died trying to escape the Great Famine. She told me how, just before her mother's death, her mother had grown melancholy thinking of the coat she'd made for her own sister who had left by ship and, only many years later, returned. Then I thought of Eily's laughter, her dancing, and the light of love that seems to shine through her face, and I smiled too.

She had offered to lodge me and fellow-traveler, Doreen Wood, at a convent run by her order. The Sisters of the St. Joseph's Order of the Sacred Heart were all nuns who had served in Australia or New Zealand. I hadn't the faintest idea what to expect. As a journalist, I had stayed in a convent in Kentucky, and interviewed Trappists—a few who were able to break their vows of silence—about their electronic scriptorium, a money-making venture to supplement their income from fruit cakes. Later I had even made a week's retreat at their Virginia monastery, staying in a spare room, practicing silence, and rising in the cold dark to hear their cycle of chants and prayers. So at the least I imagined a shared, spartan room, and a certain prohibition on alcohol and cigarettes, a potential problem for Doreen, who smokes. In the worst case, I feared an early curfew and lights out.

It was a considerable surprise, then, to have our taxi pull up at a lovely house in a smart Dublin neighborhood and to be greeted by two warm, welcoming women, Sisters Mary and Colette, wearing the modern habit of slacks and shirts adorned with crosses. "Convent living" in their home filled with comfy furniture, knick-knacks and even a big-screened T.V., especially with our private, cozy bedrooms and bath, was certainly easy to take. And when Eily arrived, we were all led to the kitchen for the ample dinner Mary had prepared. There I saw the table set in the Irish manner, with napkins stuck in the wine glasses. "Now would you prefer the red or the white, as we've both," Eily asked before turning to Doreen. "If you'd like a wee smoke after the meal, dear, then just take the ashtray into the garden. Just like my brother, God bless his soul."

After dinner, during which the three nuns regaled us with jokes, tales and stories of pioneering in the Outback and wilds of Australia and New Zealand, and what it was like to leave Ireland at seventeen with no thought of ever being able to come home again, we left with Eily. We toured the neighborhood in her car, then repaired to her apartment for a nightcap—a wee nip of the brandy.

The next day was our much-anticipated trip to Newgrange. But despite all her efforts to arrange it, Eily couldn't come. Unbelievably, at least to us Americans, she and the other Sisters of St. Joseph's Order of the Sacred Heart had been invited to a reception at the palatial home of Mary McAleese, President of the Republic of Ireland. The buzz beforehand at the convent would have been familiar to any group of women friends, including my students in Oakland: There was a flurry of phone calls about times and who was driving whom, followed by questions such as, "Should I wear the blue one or the yellow one?" and "Do you think flat shoes or low heels?"

Eventually it was all *serted* out and the nuns, suitably glamorous, traipsed off to sip champagne, nibble hors d'oeuvres, and hobnob with notables, while Doreen and I met our companions for our own day of wonders. The monument at Newgrange, built by the Boyne Valley People a thousand years before the pyramids in Egypt or the circle at Stonehenge, is a deep stone corridor beneath a grassy mound that terminates in a high alcove beneath a corbelled stone ceiling. All year it lies dark beneath the earth but for twelve days at the winter solstice. Then for seventeen minutes each day, the entire chamber fills with golden sunlight, bringing with it a sense of mystery that endures. No wonder Eily insisted I see it.

Although we hadn't toured Newgrange together, happily

my adventures with Eily were not over. My last day in Ireland we set off together for Glendanough, meaning the Valley of Two Lakes, and a site of holy ruins at the foot of the green and rugged Wicklow Mountains southeast of Dublin. We drove through woodlands, forests, mists, and intermittent rain, taking a wrong turn up a steep dirt road before finding ourselves at last at the small settlement of Celtic and early Christian ruins by the beautiful lakes. The earliest building at the monastic site is the small stone church founded by St. Kevin in the sixth century. It is surrounded by other churches, dwellings, a scriptorium, a cathedral, a monastery, towers, and tombstones overcome by grass. Most of the buildings have lost their roofs, as if to invite whatever spirits still living there to enter.

Near the ruins of ancient St. Mary's Church is a typical stone Celtic cross imbued, according to tradition as explained by Eily, with uncanny power. As she instructed me in how to hold onto it backwards, she told me what to do: "Hold on with your eyes closed until you feel its spirit, then open them to receive the sight of the hills."

Uplifted, we left to find lunch in a nearby inn, where we shared our last meal together, laughter, of course, and wine. And I received my last instruction from Sister Eily on the meaning of the spirits and the stones. "You must get in touch with the rocks and stones and sacred streams of creation," she told me, "so when that stream carries you away, you'll be ready to return to it."

A. ROLAND HOLST

※

Eighty oddish, he lives
alone in the country
not far from the sea:
two rooms, kitchen, bathroom,
his books, his music.

He received us dressed
like an Irish country gentleman
and joked about friends.
With the help of a few Genevers
I told him his old pal Frummel
called him a Cardinal in the Church
of W.B. Yeats. He replied: "Then Wolfgang's
a high priest in the Church
of Stefan Georg. But of all
Prime Ministers, Goethe
ranks the best poet."

Over his door the straw cross
Of the irish St. Brigid. We talk . . .
Later, out to dinner,
We talk poets and poetry.
He says: "I prefer Dylan Thomas
like Lament. You know,
when I was young and green
the erotic and the spiritual
walked hand in hand for me
and found harmony. With age,
the erotic faded and I feared
the spiritual would desert me too.
I was wrong. The spiritual
filled the vacuum and I've found
serenity in my last days."
He paused. "But I don't ride my beloved
Dutch bicycle anymore for fear of falling off."

After dinner, mellowed with good
gin, good wine and kitchen, we part.
He returns to two rooms, books, music,
bed, table, straw cross
and his achieved serenity.

—Desmond O'Grady

CONNECTING TO GREEN ROOTS

CONNIE GUTOWSKY

I have come to Ireland to listen, to see and to feel the meandering rivers, soft bays and wooded valleys, the green country of my father's great, great grandparents, Timothy and Mary Cullin Kelly, who emigrated to North America in 1843 from their shanty in Tipperary, County Tipperary. I've never been to this country, though I've had visions of Ireland—soda bread, spirited musicians, writers, pubs and friendly people—for as long as I can remember.

I encountered the legendary Irish warmth almost immediately, on the day after my arrival in Dublin. I had walked to the post office on O'Connell Street near Trinity College intending to buy a few stamps. If green were an emotion in Ireland it would be my eagerness—a happy tourist striding to the front and side of the post office then back again in search of the entrance. I asked the handsome policeman who stood guard in front of the old building which I'd read was designed in 1814 and renovated after being gutted in the bloody conflict of 1916, if he knew how to get in. "The entrance? It's right here," he explained. "We're standing before it. But the post office is closed today. It's Sunday." His smile came at the same time as mine, a mirror. Together we laughed.

Two days later, in County Cork, Michael O'Brien, one of our taxi drivers, takes half of our group over the many narrow lanes and winding roads in the county, past fields, farms, small cemeteries and villages in his seven seater. I often sit in the front seat, taking in the vistas of hedge-fenced green pastures, small homes and shops painted in butter-yellow, lime-green, peach, tangerine, purple, nautical blue, maroon, gray, cranberry and turquoise. I ask if urban planners regulate the artist's palette of building colors in the cities and hamlets.

"We don't say 'hamlet,' that's an English term. We say 'village' and from the time of British control, the Irish don't accept such laws. They didn't then and they don't now. The Irish use whatever color they want to paint their buildings—no regulation." I'm pleased with his answer and delighted by the landscape.

"Oh, look," says Michael, leaning over the steering wheel, laughing, "a wedding. The poor chap doesn't know what he's in for." No one says a word. We see six bridesmaids in long royal-blue satin dresses standing at a church in the distance and I comment on their round bouquets, the red hair, and the tall groomsmen. My mind goes back to a wedding at Old St.

Hilary's in Tiburon, California. I was mother of the groom. "Wear beige, say nothing," tradition dictated. I wore light violet, my own minor rebellion. I blink back to the wedding here in Ireland.

"Michael, it's Tuesday. Can people get married in church on Tuesdays?" I ask.

"People can get married any day they choose," he informs.

As we speed by on our way to lunch at the Spaniard Inn in Kinsale where we plan to meet the poet, Desmond O'Grady, Michael can't resist remarking again, "The poor man. He doesn't realize what he's in for—marrying." His laugh is a triumph.

"Says the married man," I chide.

"Yes."

Michael leans back and looks over at me with a grin.

Moments later a question comes from the back seat, "How is your little girl, Michael?"

"She has a high fever and the doctor doesn't know why. They've started a drip right into her vein." His lips close. He becomes somber. We all do. I hadn't known that his daughter was ill, and I'm struck by the contrast between Michael's good natured joke about the wedding and the seriousness of his baby's condition. I remember what my Grandfather Kelly told me the day I was married, forty-five years ago. "Do you know why people cry at weddings, Connie? It's because of everything that will happen afterwards that no one can know about now." I thought of his bit of wisdom whenever I was up all night with a sick child or whenever some trouble came. I think of it now.

Michael O'Brien worries about his six-month-old daughter, I think, just like the men in my family worry. He also teases us just like the men in my family tease. Suddenly someone asks him to explain the difference between leprechauns and faeries. "Oh," he says after his tongue touches his upper lip, "they're first cousins." And then we are off again. Michael bends close to his steering wheel, his smile is back, and I am taken by the speed of the transition.

Three days later we visit Alice Taylor, author of *To School Through the Fields*, one in a series of memoirs about Irish country life. The title reminds me of my mother, born in 1916, who showed me more than once the hilly fields where she walked two miles to a one-room school from her house in the country in Wasco County, Oregon. She shared how on very cold winter mornings, her mother hard boiled eggs and put one in each mittened hand for warmth and for lunch. On this side of the Atlantic, Alice's experiences were uncannily similar.

Alice invites all of us to her house in the village of Inishannon. The aging Irish writer is tall and lean. Her face is eager and shy, with a girlish smile revealing small, straight teeth. She wears her gray hair short with bangs. In a tailored lightweight pant suit and matching beige low-heeled slip-on shoes, she appears sensible.

"Welcome. Come in. Sit here," she beckons. We enter slowly, introduce ourselves, shake hands. We settle on her long sofa, on several comfortable straight and overstuffed chairs; two writers sit on the sturdy coffee table which has been moved to one side of the room, another sits on a tiny wooden stool. Alice sits too and talks to us about her books and those of other writers, about wanting to write to preserve a memory of life in Ireland's countryside when she was a girl, about documenting a way of life that has disappeared. I look around and think of the houses of my parents, my grandparents, my aunts and uncles in The Dalles, Oregon, where I grew up. Their houses, like Alice's, seem full of memories and give one the feeling that no problem exists that cannot be solved.

When one of our writers asks if it's true that the Irish are angry about Frank McCourt's book, *Angela's Ashes,* because it portrays life in Ireland in an unfavorable light, Alice straightens her back and speaks precisely. "No," she says, "not everyone." She suggests we read *Maura's Boys* by Christy Kinneally for another view of a poor family living in an Irish slum.

"Two men looked through prison bars. One saw mud, the other saw stars," she recites, implying both views are real. "We're very complex, aren't we?" she muses.

I agree; we are complex. Whether we leave or not we take our heritage with us, guided by the stars and the mud. We're sad and happy, resilient and vulnerable, warring and peaceful, hopeful and disheartened. We have strong views, so much like the people in the town where I grew up and the city where I live now. As I ponder her observation, it is time for us to go. I feel I could have talked with her for hours. In her quiet voice, Alice says goodbye. She walks with us toward her door where she remains, watching and waving as our bus drives past her two-story house.

I count myself fortunate. It's in these interactions that I feel my close kinship with the people of this magical isle most intensely. I'd had just such a conversation, when I first arrived, with the cabbie who drove me from Dublin airport to the Trinity Capital Hotel.

"Ya can sit in the front seat, up with me if ya like, or in the back, whichever ya choose," said Thomas Burke after he tossed my suitcase in the boot of his spotless vehicle. "Is this yar first time in Ireland?"

"Yes, it is. And I'd like to sit in front."

He opened my door. "What brings ya to Dublin?"

I told Thomas about our writers' workshop and he began to name his favorite Irish writers, starting with James Joyce. "Ya've read *Dubliners*, now, haven't ya? They made a movie about *The Dead* ya know."

I was reminded that the Irish consider their literature a critical part of every child's cultural heritage and that Irish schools expose children to the great literary works of their country from their first days in the public education system.

"And Oscar Wilde," jibes Thomas. "A wit more than a writer, he was; ya agree? And there's Seamus Heaney, the poet. Do ya write any poetry?" he asked.

"I do," I said. "Would you like to hear one of my poems?"

"I would indeed," he answered.

And so I recited the poem I called "Packing for Ireland,"

Take Joyce. Take Yeats. Take Heaney.
Take Timothy Kelly's story—
emigrant from Tipperary,
1843, your father's side.

Take love letters,
Sean O'Brien, Mairead Carey.
Take photos. Take foolery.
Take hanky.

Take tears for lost loves,
lost ancestors.
Take health. Take sun hat:
Heat's moving north.

Take memory.
The Famine. The Troubles:
The road to Ulster's
paved with doves and euros.
Take reassurance.
Take Irish breakfast tea.

"So, ya've some Irish in ya there," said the cabbie, and then he began to give me advice. "If ya take the bus, make sure ya have the right amount for the fare. If ya don't, they'll give ya a receipt and it's a lot a trouble. They don't make change so there's no theft. If it storms tomorrow, and it might, don't take the north coast tour to Malahide castle ya told me ya was goin' to take, ya wouldn't be able to see a thing."

And then we arrived at the Trinity Capital Hotel.

"I'll carry yar bag into the hotel, don't ya bother," Thomas said.

"I want to give you a tip. Please. How much is the fare?"

"Sixteen euro, and I'll take no tip from ya. Ya'll have plenty of places to spend yar money in Dublin."

We said goodbye inside the hotel.

"I hope ya enjoy Ireland," he'd said in parting.

"Thank you, Thomas Burke, I know I will."

Thomas Burke proved prescient: I do have Irish in me. And the people I met here have welcomed me home.

THE PERFECT QUOTE

(with apologies to James Joyce)

JOANNA BIGGAR

e had just arrived then, had Linda and I, in the Green Pastures of Crosshaven, as perfect a place as could be wished for the Writing Instructors and their Chief to be laying their heads, the tables always set for breakfast and all, as Connie remarked every day with a laugh (but it was always a laugh now with Connie, it has to be said) and Linda had just been telling them all, the poor green souls, the writers on the train to Cork who didn't know what they were in for, when she pronounced, Linda did, the Cardinal Rule for the writer: "Whatever you do, don't go about without notebook and pen. You might miss the very thing you need to know, maybe the perfect quote." And right she was. The writer should never be without the pen in hand, the paper, for in a whisk it could all be gone, the perfect quote, the secret to the meaning of it all.

And so it was we had just arrived in the sitting room at the Green Pastures, when Dominick, a darling twinkle of a man, all blue eyes and upbrushed hair and a mouth full of syllables from Cork, who with his sweet English wife who chats in the mornings owned the Green Pastures, came in and started talking. He said this, he said that, he said the other, who knew what he was saying all in that song-talk of Cork, until suddenly, we sat up Linda and I did. He said . . . something. The perfect quote, the key to understanding Cork and all of Ireland. "Write that down," said Linda, who just for the moment was without the pen and the paper. "Sure thing," said I, who quite by happenstance was also without the pen and the paper. Later, then, we agreed. But later, a wee sip of wine under our belt, the Writing Instructors who first thing in the day always preached the Cardinal Rule, forgot the perfect quote.

Oh, by all the saints, what were we to do, the Writing Instructors who'd broken the Cardinal Rule? How could we look them in the eye, the students, poor darlings hanging on our every word, when we had lost the perfect quote and the meaning of Cork and all of Ireland? Oh there were lamentations and gnashing of teeth, I cannot deny it, rendered more soulful by a bottle or two, and the howling of song, Connie playing drum on the table always set for breakfast, Linda swinging her hips like an Elvis impersonator, I struck dumb because (well, some things are better left unsaid) was banished to a wee chair suitable to a wee Irish Alice and not at all to the Writing Instructor that I am and song lifting the roof. Oh Hound Dog and Irish

Eyes and Hotel California and Piece of my Heart and Danny Boy and Alice's Restaurant and Pretty Woman, by God, Pretty Woman. Then heads all throbbing and eyes too big in no time it was dawn and we're again at the table always set for breakfast and Dominick all a-twinkle and his English wife who chats in the mornings asked, So who's Pretty Woman? and Linda, God bless her, couldn't remember a thing, and Connie who does indeed know how to laugh, laughed until she nearly died, and I was thinking surely there's penance to do for having lost the perfect quote and by God I'll do my best to find it and never again be without the pen and the paper in hand. And so I wasn't.

But as for the meaning of Cork and all of Ireland, I'm still searching in my fat notebook full of quotes.

I think first of the Irish Writers because if ever there were souls on Earth who know the meaning of Cork and all of Ireland it must be the writers whose tongues dance on the lovely syllables and who draw their humors from the marrow of the soil. I'm remembering the words of the rebel playwright and patriot Brendan Behan, God rest his soul, whose last words to the nursing sister in hospital in Dublin where he died of the drink were, *Sister, may all your sons be bishops.* Irish that, and moving in its way, but perhaps not the only meaning of it all. Best to turn to Alice Taylor, all soft in white, white hair, white sweater, white slacks, soft voice floating through the red-walled living room of her house in Inishannon, Cork's living memoirist telling the writers what they need to know. *Writing is like a thread to memory. It keeps going.* Aye so it is, I can't deny the truth of it, assuming of course you've the pen and the paper to write it all down. But then naturally Desmond O'Grady comes to mind, a great poet so he is, holding court at the Spaniard Inn in Kinsale, all red kerchief, hair and white eyebrows going in different directions to the eyes, seeing everything even when closed, clasping a pint like the grail, and spewing the great quotes like a fountain, faster than I can get pen to paper. *Begin at the beginning, keep going to the end.* He said this and my pen stopped dead in its tracks. He said, too, *I am Ireland.* What more meaning of it can there be?

Still there are whole other classes of Irish to consider. There would be the head gardener at the Lismore Castle where the word green doesn't begin to cover the hue of it, the carpets of grass the lofty trees the vines and bushes and the gardener, Chris Tull, himself a fine piece of nature's work, all stout and stately in the wool sweater and jeans explaining it all the castle the sculptures the Dukes and the Duchesses the rhododendrons the magnolias the rows of yew trees where Edmund Spenser wrote *The Faerie Queen*, or didn't. Then he said, Chris Tull did, *We like to make the plants feel comfortable* and I'm thinking, by God that must be it, the meaning of Ireland. Still, it might leave a few things out like the military perspective for instance. I'm thinking here of Michael the dark-haired green-eyed captain of the whale boat who with his big seafaring hands led us out of the harbor from Crosshaven into the waves of the sea, but finding no whales nor dolphins then the port and dry dock for the entire Irish Navy with its entire eight ships and he shouted out, *The Irish Navy is the only navy in the world that goes home to dinner.* By God, what a country. That could explain everything. But perhaps not the Church at least insofar as the Church is made up of the nuns like the brown-haired brown-eyed Sister Mary in Dublin fresh from New Zealand and stout in her convent apron as she prepared the stew and went on about the professor in Rangoon speaking Japanese, *the man was happy as Larry.* Which might well be the perfect quote and the key to all of Ireland and maybe Rangoon and Japan. But who's Larry?

Even reviewing the words of such notables, it's hard to go forward without researching the drivers, men of the world all. Hard to better our own Mike O'Brien the bravest of souls who fetched Connie and Linda and me from the Green Pastures at every ungodly hour laughing louder than Larry, or Connie, and spouting his wisdom at every turn, *CURLOSLYNOOSY,* he might say and something equal to follow which as God is my witness I'm positive was the perfect quote as were all the sounds to follow but I understood not a syllable of them. Still there was none better for the laugh or the song or the arousing poor Dominick tired from fetching Chinese take-away on his bike and his English wife who chats in the night too and weary from the worry of another night of the song, Pretty Woman and all. None better than Mike, but his equal would be a dark-eyed, quick-witted jack-of-all trades Irish patriot song and dance man and driver when needed who never stopped with the quotes in a land where even the ales are Catholic (Murphy's) and Protestant (Beamish). *You put a Guinness through the mouth of a cow and it comes out the other end a Murphy's indeed*, he said.

Which leads me to think that maybe the last, best, true quote would be found in a pub. Or on the way, remembering the pudding of a man who drove us from one to another in the rain, which even with the pen and the paper I swear I can't identify, the rain smearing the notes and all except the wisdom of that man's words. *Blood is t'icker than water, miss.* Hard to argue with that in Ireland, but for the thought that ale may be t'icker than blood. Or maybe the blood and the ale of the Irish do devilish work on foreigners especially mixed with a night of the music like we had at the Armada in Kinsale when that large-bellied hair-lacking fellow with few teeth stopped me on the way out.

So you're leaving then?

Yes, the buses are coming for us

Buses? They taking you back to the insane asylum.

This one I confess may not be the quote I dreamed of, but it put me in mind to think that maybe there was no going back, maybe after that fateful moment of Writing Instructor sin lacking the pen and the paper I'd lost my chance. Nobody put this quite so well as Paddy the rueful bartender at Spailpin Fanac in Cork City who said eloquently, so he did, after I mixed up my order with the Irish Mist and the Tullamore Dew, *Aye the Americans. The fecking Yanks never get it right.* Maybe not the words to unlock the meaning of Cork and all of Ireland, but in the grand scheme of things the closest to the perfect quote that I've got.

SEARCHING FOR BRACKEN'S PUB

SANDRA BRACKEN

I tried to laugh off the opening words in a poem by Greg Delanty entitled "The Fat Yanks Lament/to *the Irish-Irish*,"

> *How were any of us wiseguy kids to know*
> *when we mocked busloads of rotund Yanks*
> *bleating WOW! along every hedgerow*
> *from Malin Head to Lee banks,*
> *searching for the needle in the haystack*
> *ancestors with names like Muh-hone-ey*
> *or Don-a-hue*

Yet I soon found myself settling into a chair in writer Alice Taylor's comfortable sitting room on a rainy afternoon in

Inishannon thinking about "the needle in the haystack ancestors." She was talking quietly about the importance of being connected to times past, of knowing your ancestors. It was her children, she said, who inspired her to write her first memoir, *To School Through the Fields: An Irish Country Childhood* in 1988. It was their questions, their yearning to know about "a way of life slipping away," that started her on the path of writing it down.

She's a kindred spirit I think. I had heard in my sons the same sense of urgency when they talked about wanting to know more about the parents of their grandparents. Michael phoned one day asking for Social Security numbers and dates that I did not know.

"Why?" I asked.

He explained, "I'm going to the Library of Congress to see what information I can find about Granddaddy Wright's family."

My other son, Pete, had put together two generations of a family tree years ago and had recently renewed his questions. As a mother it seemed natural, even necessary, for me to take up their quest. It seemed prophetic, too, that the writing workshop I had chosen to take—to learn discipline and techniques to capture memories, places and journeys—was to be held in Ireland. I began a whirlwind genealogical search. But that process takes time. I didn't learn very much. I arrived in Ireland unprepared.

Then, too, I might never be able to fill in all the gaps. I would have to rely on luck, on serendipity. Preparing for the trip, I carried around the poems of Greg Delanty. I wanted to believe his words in another poem:

> *As our mainland*
> *world diminishes*
> *there is respite.*
> *A cloud engulfs us*
> *out of nowhere*
> *as if the miraculous*
> *were about to appear.*

It might require a miracle to uncover the information I was hoping for: names on a list, a building, a grave stone.

I envy the families of Irish heritage who have a clear path of lineage. Surprisingly, in our case it was the Brackens, my husband's family, who yielded the best information. I had just arrived in Ireland, and walked through the door of my guest house in Dublin. Immediately, Noel Comer, the perceptive owner, was talking about how important it is to know your heritage, "especially for sons," he enthused. I had not uttered a word and could only nod approvingly. I was grateful for that moment of reassurance. He introduced me to the chef, Delia, née Bracken. She primed my optimism with her own eagerness. Her eyes sparkled as she told me of her home town and Bracken's Pub there. Before I knew it, I was on the train to Tullamore in County Offaly.

Immigration records show that my husband's ancestor Peter

Bernard Bracken left County of Kings (now County Offaly) in 1850, and settled in Kings County, New York. Walking down the neat and tidy busy main street and by the Grand Canal, Tullamore seemed a town proud and sure of itself. But the only pub I found was Loughrey's. In the process though, I met many people who were cheerfully willing to spend ten minutes helping me. One young woman phoned her husband on her cell phone.

"He's more familiar with the pubs than I am!" she laughed. I had been in Ireland only one day and already felt comfortable, connected.

While it had been somewhat easy to gather information about my husband's family, mine proved more difficult. They were farmers in Virginia. Few written records seem to have been kept or have survived. The surnames haunt me: Wright, McCallister, Clarke. Who were the first to arrive and when? Where in Ireland did they come from? My father believed that his great-grandfather came from County Cork. I, unfortunately, had not been able to find any documents to verify that. County Cork was my ultimate destination on this trip for several reasons. Our writers' workshop was based there and had an ambitious itinerary well-suited to my personal quest. Daily excursions took us to many corners of the county, through small towns from Mizen Head to Youghal to Lismore and included visits with writers and poets and evenings of music in local pubs.

I was most curious about the city of Cobh. As a port city, it has a long history of ships crossing the Atlantic, from the earliest steamship, *Sirius,* to the emigration ships to the *Lusitania* and *Titanic,* that also sailed from there.

"Go on a grey day and the sense of loss is still almost palpable," my guide book said. It was raining when we pulled up to the renovated Victorian train station that has been converted into a Heritage Centre. As I walked into the darkened halls I was indeed wrapped in the emotions of another time. Standing in front of the wall of words describing an "American Wake," tears welling, I read: ". . . a party was often held on the emigrant's last night at home when a mixture of gaiety and sorrow marked their departure. Food, drink, music, dancing, songs and reminiscences carried on 'til morning. The wake grew out of the tradition of waking (watching) the dead. The likelihood of the emigrant not returning meant that they were dead to those left behind. Friends and relatives accompanied them at least part of the way to the port. The group would travel to a certain point along the road or to the nearest station where the final sad leave taking would take place. Home, family and friends were never seen again." I was not prepared for this bit of reality.

I do not know when the Clarkes or McAllisters arrived in Virginia, whether in the eighteenth or nineteenth century. I do not know if they left as a direct result of the Famine, the failure of the potato crop between 1845 and 1851, or if members of their families were counted in the million deaths at that time. It is said more than 2.5 million Irish emigrated from Cobh.

I forced myself to focus on other reasons that might have motivated those who made that difficult decision. In addition to crop failure and the resulting poverty, the land system would have been reason enough to want to leave. But those planning the trip must have been dreaming of what might be possible in another country. Somehow that unknown place and life would seem better, brighter.

Peter B. Bracken owned a stable in New York within ten years of his arrival there. His son owned a saloon. Another son was a Pinkerton man. The Clarkes and McAllisters eventually bought their own farms in Virginia. One such piece of land is still in the family. I believe great optimism combined with greater stubbornness saw them through the difficulties they encountered. And I see myself as a successful outcome of their struggles.

The Cobh exhibit stated that 46 million British pounds were sent back to Ireland in fifty years. Alice Taylor also mentioned the money sent back to families and talked about those who did return, if ever so briefly. They were honored.

"All routine activity would be suspended during the time of the visit," she said. In her first book, there is a chapter on Nell, the youngest member of a large family, who lived alone, yet had no financial worries. Her entire family had gone to America, "and done well and . . . when they died Nell was the beneficiary."

Not having enough family information to successfully use the genealogical records at the Heritage Centre was a disappointment. No miracle was waiting for me there. I did learn that there are many such centers throughout the country, that Ireland seems to be one giant genealogical resource.

All the while I was looking at people, talking with some, and wondering about some distant genetic connection. I fell into conversation with Desmond, a silversmith, in his workshop, also sales room. His sincere love of his craft and his enjoyment in sharing his knowledge with a stranger reminded me of my older son. But I suspect it was his intense, yet gentle, gaze that drew me to him. The chattiest people I met were taxi drivers, who helped me with seeming delight. One of them could have been my other son, talking passionately about Irish football, and proudly about his two sons and his hopes for a daughter, as his wife was pregnant. He was even sorry he didn't have an extra ticket to give me for the weekend game.

In pubs, I sat in a corner enjoying my Murphy's, soaking up the conviviality, letting myself sink into the mood and the music and wondering—could that be Linn from Maryland on the *uilleann* pipes or Pete on the guitar? At Buckley's in Crosshaven, I watched Nina, competent, engaging, always smiling, manage the overflow crowd on a Monday night. We hugged each other all around as she held the door open for us at the end of the night. I thought of my grandmother's mother, Bettie McAllister, how well she ran the little country store with her husband, how good she was with customers, even pumping their gas. More importantly, she gave her great-granddaughters their choice of penny candy and bagged it with a smile and added a secure hug when saying good-bye.

The road in front of our B&B ends some miles away at Sunfield Farm. It is identified by a small, almost hidden handwritten sign. On one sunny morning a farmer was coming out of the lane as I was walking by. He, slightly muddied in work clothes and Wellingtons, and I, obviously a visitor, exchanged "good mornings"—a simple, common enough event, except for what I was thinking. The ghosts of my ancestors seemed to breathe in everyone I met. I was somewhat bewildered by being caught up in a yearning, a spell the country, Ireland, weaves. I didn't have to know the cottage or town my ancestors lived in. I just needed to float through, feel the air, touch the earth and hear the voices. I realized the miraculous is a state of mind.

I won't give up my genealogical search. I'll intensify my efforts. I will tell my sons to come with me to Ireland next time. Perhaps we'll find that corner of County Cork where the McAllisters farmed a piece of land. I know that together we will find Bracken's Pub. Or if not Bracken's, then Wrights's, Clarke's or McAllister's.

Pangur Bán

Barbara J. Euser

Wending my way through the exhibition at the Book of Kells, I stopped short at the ceiling-high panel of a poem.

> *I and Pangur Bán, my cat*
> *'Tis a like task we are at;*
> *Hunting mice is his delight*
> *Hunting words I sit all night.*
>
> *Better far than praise of men*
> *'Tis to sit with book and pen;*
> *Pangur bears me no ill will,*
> *He too plies his simple skill.*

'Tis a merry thing to see
At our tasks how glad are we,
When at home we sit and find
Entertainment to our mind.

Oftentimes a mouse will stray
In the hero Pangur's way:
Oftentimes my keen thought set
Takes a meaning in its net.

'Gainst the wall he sets his eye
Full and fierce and sharp and sly;
'Gainst the wall of knowledge I
All my little wisdom try.

When a mouse darts from its den,
O how glad is Pangur then!
O what gladness do I prove
When I solve the doubts I love!

So in peace our tasks we ply,
Pangur Bán, my cat, and I;
In our arts we find our bliss,
I have mine and he has his.

Barbara J. Euser ⊗ Pangur Bán

Practice every day has made
Pangur perfect in his trade;
I get wisdom day and night
Turning darkness into light.

Unable to memorize it on the spot, I bought a copy at the bookstore on the way out. Many have translated this poem from Gaelic and it has been alternately attributed to a student, a scholar, or a monk. Seamus Heaney's translation entitled "Pangur Bán" begins,

Pangur Bán and I at work,
Adepts, equals, cat and clerk:
His whole instinct is to hunt,
mine to free the meaning pent.

Frank O'Connor's translation entitled "The Scholar and the Cat" begins,

Each of us pursues his trade,
I and Pangur my comrade,
His whole fancy on the hunt,
And mine for learning ardent.

The full translation above—the one I love—is by Robin Flower, entitled "The Student and His Cat." The anonymous author of the poem immortalized his work on the margins of a copy of the Epistles in the ninth century. He was working at St. Paul's Monastery on Reichenau Island in Lake Constance (Bodensee), where Germany borders Carinthia, Austria. I was surprised to learn that this favorite Irish poem was actually written in Austria. But as I began to learn about the history of Irish-founded monasteries, it wasn't surprising at all.

Irish monasteries had developed into great centers of scholarship in the 500s CE. By the 600s, there were dozens of monasteries, some as large as Clonard, Bangor and Clonfert with 3,000 or more monks each. Others comprised hundreds of monks. In contrast to other branches of the Catholic Church, the Irish Church was "in the world," serving its congregants. St. Augustine and St. Martin of Tours had expressed a similar concept: monks were the servants, not the masters, of their flock.

Irish monasteries were based on the principle of self-support: they raised their own food and did not rely on gifts or taxes from the local population. In addition to copying manuscripts for distribution, they provided free education to local children as well as those of the affluent aristocracy. Children were schooled from ages seven to seventeen: the first son and the first daughter in a family were accepted. Some—but not all—of the children of a family might receive an education. Most students were expected to return to secular life after completing their education. They became bi-lingual in Latin and studied Greek; poems, stories and laws were taught in Gaelic. Foreigners traveled from abroad to study in Ireland.

The monastic centers of learning produced advances in

mechanical engineering, botany, zoology and agronomy. The latter included such apparently mundane advances as plows with metal collars, as well as sophisticated methods of harnessing water power, which allowed the expansion of arable land. The monasteries became the centers of agricultural communities. Population around the monasteries increased as they attracted craftsmen and artisans, metalworkers and carvers, painters and goldsmiths. Each monastery included a scriptorium for the copying of manuscripts.

But the unfortified monasteries were subject to attack from the sea, first from Irish clan barons, then from the Vikings, who looted, burned manuscripts and sometimes murdered the monks. In the late sixth century, the emigration of Irish monks began. In 565, Columba traveled to Scotland to establish monasteries. Fifteen years later, his friend, compatriot and fellow poet Columban traveled with twelve disciples to establish monasteries in France and the rest of Europe. In addition to founding monasteries, both Columba and Columban made significant innovations in poetry.

Before his death in 615, Columban and his immediate followers, eventually amounting to several thousand monks from Ireland, established forty monasteries on the Continent. They used the same teaching methods they had developed at home. From the standpoint of education, the period from 500-800 has been described as a "mass-literacy movement." As they had in Ireland, the monks taught Latin and Greek and also created dictionaries, compiling words and expressions so they could teach in local vernacular languages, French, German, and Italian. Between 575 and 725, the Irish monastic movement founded one hundred and thirteen monasteries and schools in France and Switzerland, twenty-six in Germany, ten in Austria and three in the north of Italy.

The monasteries were schools and the schools were scriptoria, from which new copies of the Scriptures and other religious writings were dispersed throughout Europe. The student, scholar, or monk who wrote Pangur Bán found himself in just such a scriptorium in the 800s.

He was not the only copyist to write in the margins of the manuscript upon which he was working. Kuno Meyer translated "The Blackbird," written by a monk in the margin of a book he was copying in the seventh century:

> *Ah, blackbird, thou art satisfied*
> *Where thy nest is in the bush:*
> *Hermit that clinkest no bell,*
> *Sweet, soft, peaceful is thy note.*

Of religious significance, a nine verse poem was found in the margin of a ninth century Latin Juvencus manuscript. Six of the nine verses are explicitly trinitarian, that is, containing a reference to the Holy Trinity. This is the earliest example of the trinitarian poetic tradition written in Welsh. The books being copied were important, but the poems in the margins are also an important legacy.

Just one day after visiting the Book of Kells in Dublin, a friend and I found ourselves in Kinsale, taking refuge from the rain in the Armada pub. Two musicians held forth, an Irish folk singer playing the guitar and a drummer. We joined the enthusiastic crowd, clapping and singing along whenever we could. Later, the singer joined us. We complimented him on his repertoire.

He graciously thanked us, then informed us that folk singing was not his greatest interest. His greatest interest was bringing Celtic culture into the lives of Irish youth. He takes ancient Celtic rhymes and turns them into modern music: rap. He pulled a set of keys out of his pocket, closed them lightly in his fingers and, shaking the keys, established the beat. He began rapping,

> *I and Pangur Bán my cat,*
> *Tis a like task we are at:*
> *Hunting mice is his delight,*
> *Hunting words I sit all night...*

KINSALE

❀

Cúin tSaile or Ceann tSaile:
Quiet of the Sea or Head of the Ocean.
Either way, home-haven. Here we all
live blow-ins: exiles, or exiles from
exile. And we love our ease, our idleness.
You would too if you lived here among us.

The Bandon river finds sea exit here,
Atlantic spawning salmon entrance,
Kinsale origins flowered beyond the ice sphere
which makes Time and History a nonsense.
Here Celtic alternative order fought, died,
sixteen one; left us Ireland's modern divide.

We sleep side by side, together,
enjoying harmony's just measure
without weapons on display for war.

—DESMOND O'GRADY

Sláinté

Doreen Wood

The fabled conviviality of Irish pubs was about to become a reality for me on that bone-wet night in Myrtleville, County Cork, Ireland. Several years ago I'd had a great personal loss followed by many lonely nights and I'd longed for gatherings around a big round kitchen table. Now, bright blue eyes stared at me as I pushed open the rough-hewn door of the Pine Lodge pub. I was cold and the luminescent swinging "Murphy's" sign had beckoned me as I'd abruptly left my walking companions. I must have been a sight, with my wind-blown platinum hair and my cheeks freshly pinked atop my shimmering ruby raincoat. Fifteen men looked at me as if I were a phenomenon they were going to thoroughly enjoy.

"Well, well, come in," called the red-haired man perched on the bar stool nearest the doorway. "Sit down."

I didn't yet know that any unfamiliar face in this neighborhood would be looked at with concerted interest, or as I came to call it, gleeful scrutiny.

Another broad-faced man called out, "You one of the bunch of writers staying up the hill? They told us some of you might be stopping by."

Someone else piped up, "Just for a sec there we thought you might be a *banshee*."

I stammered, "Yes, yes, we just got here this afternoon. We're supposed to look for Irish stories."

"Well we can give you stories," chimed in yet another jovial character. "From America, you are. So, sure. See those two guys huddling at the end of the bar? They're a gay couple, but no one can tell for sure. And see the fellow sitting at the little round table over there? He's having an affair with my wife's best friend, but it's a secret!"

And so the bantering went on. Accepting their gift of a hot toddy, I raised my glass and my new friends chimed "*Slainté.*" Thoroughly warmed, I made my retreat back up the hill to the B&B.

I thought often about that welcoming first night as for the following ten days our hosts introduced us to numerous pubs with music that was beautiful, spirited, and alive. At the Armada pub in the town of Kinsale in County Cork we met such a happy scene. Here, Tuesday nights are always "round table" nights where musicians, who don't usually play together, gather around a large, scarred oak table and play whatever comes into their hearts. On that particular Tuesday we were treated by Iain, toasting his third new baby with his guitar, Joivmuid with his banjo, Sean and his accordion, and John Paul with his pennywhistle. We tapped our feet in delight and joy as we listened to their lively jigs. We learned that Joivmuid and Sean were buskers, the musicians, poets and mimes that entertain the mingling crowds along the length of O'Connell Street in Cork City. Kevin, a burly longshoreman with a grin as wide as his long blond ponytail, joined them later with his big pennywhistle. Even Gail Strickland, the musician in our group, picked up the guitar and charmed us with a French folk song.

In Cork City, we had another whimsical musical pub experience at the Spailpin Fanac, right beside the Beamish & Crawford Brewery. Two wooden flutes entranced us for several hours with interlacing ballads, the atmosphere bringing on conversation with ease. Nursing a wine cooler, I sat toward the back of the brick-walled rectangular room with a member of my group, lovely-eyed Connie Gutowsky, my body and spirit relaxing as the gentle tunes twined with the gregariousness of the more boisterous patrons in the outer room.

Two nights before we left County Cork, we stopped at Buckley's in Crosshaven, a town just a stone's throw from our B&B. We were treated to an overflowing profusion of music, and quite an evening that was. A shot of Jameson's whiskey appeared on the table in front of me, and a down-home bit of Ireland materialized in the form of water in a thick pottery jug emblazoned with green shamrocks. Not long after, another jug appeared for me with the message, "Here's a gift from the owner."

The music became livelier and more spirited. I jumped up, ordered another warming shot of whiskey and tapped the soft shoulder of a round blond woman sitting at the bar. She nimbly hopped off her stool and the two of us danced like a couple of whirling dervishes. Interspersed with two more shots of Jameson's, I skipped and twirled, until Buckley's closed, and I spun my way into the waiting car.

In the morning as I nursed my dull headache, a member of my group was stern with me, "I was counting and you had four shots of that whiskey."

My Dutch colleague's retort, "You had a great time. You should have thought more quickly and told her you'd had six shots!"

My wild evening gave me a sense of what we bring into our pub experiences. Whether a myth or a historical reality, Ireland has long had a reputation for heavy imbibing and it's probably true that, for some, alcohol has provided an emigration of the soul. I'd been reminded of that possibility when I was in Dublin the week before I traveled south to County Cork. I'd stopped into the Berkeley, a neighborhood pub on Mountjoy Street, a side street off the main O'Connell Street in Dublin. I'd gone into the pub for a glass of wine before heading to my spartan sleeping space at the International Hostel across the street. It was warm in the small dark-paneled room, the musty aromas of stout and lager wafting in the dim space. Sitting at a miniscule table in the corner, I watched the five men hunched on the bar stools, jumpers or sweaters nestled on their collarbones, elbows simultaneously resting on the smooth wood of the bar, each with their right forearms bent, a curved handclasp on their thick glass mugs of beer. All were listening to the one-sided phone conversation of bartender Gerald, a gray-striped apron over his tan shirt.

"Oh Frank, miss ye, and miss ye . . ."

"In the hospital, aye . . .?"

"Three days now . . ."

"Told ye to drop the drink, aye . . .?"

"Well, see you in here soon's ye get out . . ."

The men's pale faces do not react. They hear the news of their compatriot, even though the dim lights of the pub flicker for an instant.

Mottle-cheeked Paddy, third from the left, raised his empty mug, "Let's have one on Frank!"

That somber pub seemed to mirror my own experiences of bars in my own early life in Winnipeg, Canada in the 1950s when my mother had often sent me to the beer parlor two blocks away to collect my father to come home for supper. If he was working and had just been paid, he'd have likely bought a fresh round for all the others.

But I'd stand in the doorway anyway, calling, "Daddy, Daddy."

As we were getting ready to leave Ireland, Ann Ure, her eyes twinkling at the prospect of a bit more fun, came along with me to stop in again at the Pine Lodge pub in Myrtleville. I wanted to bid this genial neighborhood assemblage farewell and thank them for my witty pub introduction. This time, it was a bit earlier, and a Friday evening, so some young children were running around and there were some clusters of women. Ann and I ordered mugs of dark stout and she immediately became involved in animated conversation with Steve Kelley, a stonemason who loves horses, and Frank McAdam, a dry cleaner who's been coming here every Friday night for fourteen years.

I moved over to the broad doorway to talk to the women.

Breda Cotter, an attractive woman in her forties with streaked blond hair, was spending the weekend at her summer home high up on the hill and was nursing a wine cooler. "Oh, how my sister loves to meet Americans!" she declared. "Please come for tea tomorrow and I'll get her over here."

And Katt McInnis, a tall curly-haired lass, was passing out invitations to her fortieth birthday party.

"Come, come," she laughed. "It's on July twenty-first and it's a costume party; you have to come dressed as a bride or a punk. I figure that at forty I'm never going to be a bride so I'm certainly coming dressed as a punk. We're going to have a band and lots and lots of food." Katt, who is Cork's open-air tour bus driver, implored me to come into the city for a free city tour.

It did seem that wherever we went, I ended up in a pub. Earlier in the week, after a full day of touring, including a leisurely stroll through the magnificent Lismore Castle gardens, we ended up in the town of Lismore, on the main route to

Killarney via the picturesque Blackwater Valley. Our finale for the day was to watch a forty-five minute audio-visual presentation at the Lismore Heritage Centre on Main Street, but all I wanted was a cup of coffee to revive myself. Directed to the pub in the hotel across the street, and expecting the usual comfy atmosphere, I set myself down at the gleaming bar, its chrome appliances sparkling in the immaculate room.

"Yes," the bar-person informed me. "We'll serve you a cup of coffee." She was dressed in an ironed white shirt under a waistcoat and wore neatly pressed black pants. Looking around, I saw that all four workers wore a similar uniform.

I thought to myself, "I can hardly believe that I've ended up in another pub. But this one is different. This is upscale, chic."

People spoke in modulated tones about the ancient Celtic game of hurling. Nora, the bar-woman, politely explained to me that there'd been a big contest just that day between Cork and Waterford Counties. Though it was pleasant, I hope that with Ireland's prosperity, and it's Celtic Tiger identity, the congeniality and down-home comfort of a traditional Irish pub isn't going to go by the wayside.

It's hardly likely. Since the seventeenth century, men—women's presence only being fully accepted since the 1960s—have come to the pubs. For instance, for older bachelors from farms on the sides of the mountains, visits to the pub were a necessary part of their social fabric. For some, alcohol provided an escape from their reality of poverty, but many never kept a drink in the house. They came to relax and unwind, to meet friends, to eat and drink, whether with a cup of coffee, beer, or whiskey. To this day, people know that there are no expectations, that they can show up and be accepted. I realize that what I found and loved so much about the Irish pubs was conviviality, companionship and community. I'd found my round kitchen table here, where people raise their glasses in good-natured Irish cheer, "*Slainté!*"

Courting Daisy

Ann Kathleen Ure

Fritz wasn't the best-looking guy in the seaside village of Myrtleville, but he was the first one I met. He gazed at us from the lawn of the B&B as we pulled up. Friendly yet cautious, he approached and greeted our group of writers in a rather perfunctory manner. He avoided making direct eye contact with me, though it was obvious that he sized up each one of us before returning to his post at the edge of the lawn beside the inn's lovely dining veranda.

Fritz wore his reddish brown hair short. Relatively young, there were telltale flecks of white in his eyelashes and beard indicating that he'd been around the block a few times. He also appeared to be a bit scraggly, but in that way that the Irish can work unkempt to their advantage. Despite his stern demeanor and rather short stature, I immediately found him attractive.

"What's his story?" I asked the proprietor.

"That's Fritz," he said with a sigh and a shake of his head. "He's from Fennell's Bay, about two miles down the road. He hangs about more than we like, but he's okay."

I didn't understand, and continued my probe. "You say he hangs about your property?"

"Yes. He's in love with our Daisy," Benny replied, "but she's not the least bit interested in him. I guess he's not her type."

"What's Daisy's type?" I asked, my curiosity having been tweaked.

"The big guys," he confided, "Labrador retrievers, mostly."

Daisy, whom I was to meet a few moments later, was a Jack Russell terrier, like Fritz. She had blond hair, reddish spots and bright, dark brown eyes. I also knew that she had a lot of spunk given the information that she preferred the "big guys." Daisy stood a petite eleven inches in height with legs very generously estimated at four inches in length. But, as they say, size doesn't really matter and, at least to young Fritz, Daisy was clearly the canine queen of this castle. Ah, puppy love. It could only have been made sweeter had Daisy returned Fritz's affections.

I have always been drawn to love stories: fulfilled, unrequited, and even the four-legged varieties so romantically anthropomorphized in Walt Disney movies. I enjoy reliving the budding and struggling relationship between Elizabeth Bennett and Mr. Charles Darcy in *Pride and Prejudice*. I tear up when Juliet awakens and takes her life before Romeo is revived. I am gratified when I see young Heidi bond with her crotchety, old grandfather. Frankly, I am touched when I witness compatibilities of any kind, at any time, any place, and within any species.

There was no shortage of love stories to be found here in Ireland. Centuries-old Irish tales, real and imagined, were present in abundance, including stories of kings with their queens, and of fair princes coming to the aid of damsels in distress. But not all of these tales ended on high notes.

Just outside of Carrigaline on the drive to West Cork, for example, we spotted a larger-than-life-sized white horse painted on the side of an immense cliff with a castle perched on its crest. This was legendary Ballea Castle, built on a rock in the sixteenth century.

The story goes that the daughter of the lord of Ballea Castle frequently rode a white horse to hunt where she met, then fell in love with the son of a local farmer. Returning from the hunt one day, she told her father of her intention to marry the young man. Her father strongly disapproved of the match and shouted at his daughter, raising his riding crop as if to strike her. As a result, her frightened horse bolted over the cliff's edge and horse and rider plunged to their deaths. Her contrite father had the horse painted upon the side of the cliff. The painting of the horse had been maintained ever since to immortalize the ill-fated lovers.

The tale behind the magnificent rendering of the white horse beneath Ballea Castle was definitely the most chilling example of a tragic love story that I heard while in County

Cork. I observed other physical signs of lost love, too, though more contemporary in nature—such as the tattoo "to Maureen, my one and only, forever," on the arm of a local man now married to someone else. His body art reminded me of my own wounds from love gone awry. Luckily, my scars were only psychological.

Looking further back into Irish lore, I found additional tales of frustrated and unrequited love. Caer, the fairy maiden of Connacht, caught my attention when I learned that she lived in the guise of a swan. Her father played along with her penchant for dress-up. And so, even when Angus, the Irish God of Love, asked for her hand, her father responded by sending him down to the lake to see if he could pick her out of the flock. According to the tale, Angus recognized fair Caer immediately. But rather than rewarding him by transforming back into a maiden, Caer transformed Angus into a swan. At least they flew off together.

Personally, I've never adopted feathers nor ridden off a cliff for love, but I've certainly weathered my fair share of romantic ups and downs. I remember one young man, Tim, who thought I was the cat's meow, though I hadn't set out to charm him. In those days I was the popular Daisy but my taste ran to the slight, dark, mysterious guys, and Tim was a big, friendly guy over six feet tall, blond and muscular.

Years later, Tim and his physique would be right up my alley, especially if he'd thrown in a beard for good measure. Tim treated me like a lady and intimated that his mother would really like me, too. But I wasn't having it during the year he

184

took a fancy to me. How ironic that I once perceived such sensitive sentiments and behavior as turn-offs.

I have also played the Fritz role on occasion. When I was a college co-ed I pined for my own Irish lad. His name was Michael and he had bright red hair, freckles and round wire-rim glasses á la John Lennon. I wore round wire-rim glasses then too—a sure sign that we were meant to be.

Michael and I were in the same English Lit class. I thought everything he said was brilliant. Our unrequited love story consisted of a few conversations, lunch on the quad, and my borrowing a book he referenced in class. I didn't read it but I fingered the pages and tucked it under my pillow the night before I returned it to him. The infatuation concluded when I saw Michael cozying up to another girl who had her own pair of Lennon wire-rims. I determined that there would be plenty of other boys to adore, so I was only slightly heartbroken. In fact, the only other thing I remember about my mooning-over-Michael period was that he burped very loudly when he drank a Coke.

Though I never came close to being a stalker, I could see shades of that behavior in Fritz whom I observed dogging Daisy on more than one occasion. Every morning and evening she'd scurry out the back door of the B&B and down the stairs to the lane with Fritz on her tail. Though she never stopped to respond to his attempts at foreplay, she tolerated him. It was as if he was a constant reminder that she still "had it" even though she didn't "want it."

These pooches were quite the pair: running in tandem, of the same height, and having identical peaked ears that bent to form small cornered flaps over their very expressive faces. One looked very much the same as the other except Fritz was bulkier and sweet Daisy had a slight limp. Their compatible patterns reminded me of another wonderful Irish faery tale titled "The Queen of the Lonely Isle." It was very Fritz and Daisy up until the final paragraph.

In this story the King of Donegal met and fell in love with the Queen from the Isle of Loneliness. On a trip away from his home he encountered the Queen in the form of an old lady, but he saw through to her inner beauty. They fell in love and married and might have lived happily ever after had he not made a return trip to Donegal to share the news of his match.

Unfortunately, once out of her sight the King promptly forgot her, and it took him years and years and a magic trick or two before he was reminded that he had a wife and a son waiting for him back on the island. From the Queen's perspective, this definitely counted as a fair bit of unrequited love if not outright abandonment. In fact, he was pretty darn lucky that she continued to carry a torch for him when he finally got his wits back. And take him back, she did.

By the week's end, I was able to watch the daily dance between Fritz and Daisy with greater distance and perspective. I concluded that Fritz, frustrated as he seemed to be, enjoyed more than a modicum of Daisy's attentions and had accepted his role as perennial suitor. In a photograph of the two of them trotting up the driveway, side by side, they appear more like an old married couple than a pair of ill-fated lovers—perhaps the transformed and reunited Queen of the Lonely Isle with her King. Except in this version of the story the King's amorous advances were forever doomed to be met with a low growl and a woof—the firm but gentle canine equivalent of "no, dear, not tonight."

PUB

❈

Young fellows, faces
like stars at night,
rattled the table
for more drink.

Night wrapped round us
like a satin mantle.
I took them to a pub
of a man I know.

Knock on the door,
the special knock.
he opened a knuckleworth.
Pause. Then: "Who's that?"
"Nobody you'd know who never
takes no for an answer."

He laughed: "I'm a friend of nobody
and nobody's been here all night."
He opened. We settled inside.
He produced a bottle from the back
of the shop no man had seen before.
She was so wrapped up she looked
like a girl veiled in her bed, fit
for the eyes of the fervent few.

That eunuch the curate poured her
and charmed us with his curate
talk and his one gold earring.

But time won't leave us in peace
till it upends everything
and shunts us home to bed.

after Abu Nuwas
(Iraq c. 747-815 CE)

—DESMOND O'GRADY

189

ALL ABOARD IN CORK HARBOR

LINDA WATANABE MCFERRIN

Gale force winds, rain, twenty-six-foot seas—we'd hit a bit of a rough spot in the weather on the Irish Riviera, the tourist board's somewhat euphemistic appellation for the strip of resort towns—Youghal, Ardmore, Dungarvan, Cobh and Ballycotton—that dot Ireland's southern coast and draw travelers to their lovely beaches and coastlines. Not that this put a damper on our adventures. My travel companions and I had spent most of our days in landlubberly pursuits, crawling all over the Cork County countryside, grinning from ear to ear, traipsing through museums and gardens and markets, nattering away at the locals with our incessant questions, supping famously and excessively in restaurants, guzzling liters and liters of brown beer in pubs, and hobnobbing with poets and writers and artists and musicians anywhere we could find them.

Rain or shine, we were having a super time.

In Cobh we filed, soggy as Seattle's morning edition, into the Cobh Heritage Centre where we "oohed" and "aahed" at the exhibits and stuffed ourselves on cakes and cream before heading out to the foot of the Knockmealdown Mountains in County Waterford and the banks of the River Blackwater. There, in Lismore, we spent a sparkling afternoon at majestic Lismore Castle touring the elegant gardens under the guidance of master gardener, Chris Tull. We'd hugged the druidic stones in West Cork at the Drombeg Stone Circle and jiggled and bounced along on a seemingly endless bus ride down the Mizen Head Peninsula to the Fastnet Lighthouse, clip-clopping under stormy skies across the suspension bridge that connects the small island from which the lighthouse rises to the mainland. Gannets whirled above the rocky cliffs, boats circled in the waters far below. The outlook over the wide Atlantic from Mizen Head was inspiring, moving some to spontaneous poetic discourse and stunning others finally into silence. It was the perfect culmination of a long cross-country excursion through garden and wood, across field and stream, to lands' end and the very brink of the isle. All well and good, but I had a hankering for a sea voyage of some kind.

After all, there we were, staying in Crosshaven on the Corkish coast, Cork Harbor being the second largest natural harbor in the world and Ireland's second largest port. To my mind, as a person who'd memorized most of the words to the *Little Mermaid* as a girl, and as a lover of waterlogged tales like

Titanic (the great ship set sail on that tragic last journey from Cork Harbor on April 11, 1912, only to be struck by an iceberg three days later about 400 miles southeast of Cape Race, Newfoundland), *Poseidon Adventure, The Perfect Storm* and—weirdly—*The Secret of Roan Inish* or, as it is known in novel form, *The Secret of Ron Mor Skerry*, this was a part of the Irish environment that I did not want to miss. Besides I've always been drawn to the sea and its mysteries. Not in the cruise-ship-all-you-can-eat kind of way, but in more of a Rhyme-of-the-Ancient-Mariner-Mutiny-on-the-Bounty-tough-time-but-great-story style. Put me on a Ranger 88 heading out to the guano-encrusted, curlew- and puffin-infested Farallon Islands and I'm happy. Send me off on a 128-foot Islander to explore the 24,000 islands and skerries of the Stockholm Archipelago and I'm in heaven. Heck, you can press me into service navigating the locks on the Canal du Midi, deflate my banana boat in the middle of the Pacific, even stick me in a canoe in a swamp and make it capsize, and I'll be an ecstatic explorer. I live very close to a lake in a coastal city, am crazy about tide pools and aquariums; I even married a fish, for God's sake. Well, maybe not a fish, but a swimmer.

To top it all off, I'd broken my ankle a few months before and was still nursing my new metal parts. Long hikes were out, no matter how alluring the prospect, so a day on the high seas seemed ideal to me, and we'd actually planned for one on my birthday.

I don't know if it was Barbara or Connie who contacted

Whale of a Time, an adventure boating company operating from Castletownshend just east of Skibbereen, that takes clients out on harbor, river and coastal trips along the southern shores of Ireland. Michael Hallahan and his partner, Kevin Higgins, have been running these trips for three years, though Michael has been on the sea since 1984. On Mischief, his eleven-meter Redbay Enclosed Rib, we could motor out, nine at a time, for a number of hours in search of some of the marvelous marine life that inhabits Irish waters.

In the early 1990s, in response to a proposal made by the Irish Whale and Dolphin Group, the Irish government declared its coastal waters a whale and dolphin sanctuary, the first of its kind in Europe. Well over twenty species of cetaceans have been recorded on the western and southern perimeter of the island, along with the shoals of small fish that support them. Massive fin, humpback and minke whales of the baleen persuasion are regular visitors to the waters in these parts, upstaged occasionally by smaller, predatory odontoceti such as the killer whale or orca. In addition, several species of delphinidae like to sport in the area including, some say, a resident pod of bottlenose dolphins. Of course there are seals, conger eels, rays, all manner of fish, and plenty of peckish sea birds cruising the skies in constant search of a snack. A promising cast of characters for any sea-loving soul—we were bound to encounter these locals.

Sadly the weather was against us. Our first trip was cancelled as the seas were too nasty and the weather decidedly bad, but on July 1, rough seas or not, we set out from Crosshaven, home of the world's oldest yacht club, for our own little whale of a time.

We had high hopes for the day. The kind and solicitous lady of the manor at the bed and breakfast where most were staying, had wisely provided handfuls of cloves to be tucked into mouths to ward off sea-sickness—an old, natural preventative—though I suspect their best use is to sweeten the breath once the terrible moment has passed. Our skipper and his first mate, a sunburned, Andy Richter look-alike, buckled us up into car seat-like contraptions: life jackets with crotch straps to ensure that our water wings wouldn't be going anywhere without us once we were in the drink. Ann, Chrysa, Mary Jean, Connie G., Annelize and Joanna all decided to hang out with Andy-boy on the stern, while I took a seat next to our captain, inside, in the front of the boat.

Mike said we'd try to head south around twenty miles in search of minke whales. There was also the pod of resident bottlenose dolphins at the harbor mouth that he hoped we'd see, but as the boat pitched and rolled, he explained that conditions might make it difficult to locate them.

"How high are these waves?" I asked, as what looked like a green wall of glass rose before us.

"Around twelve to fourteen feet," said Mike, angling the boat to catch the wave's crest and ride it for a time before dipping back into the deep trough alongside it. A fine spray washed in through the window.

"Wow, that was cool."

He smiled, expertly maneuvering the craft to skim one vitreous wall after another, his pale green eyes moving quickly to mine before turning back to the far more absorbing sight of the wide gray horizon. I settled in to pepper him with my innumerable questions.

Meanwhile, on deck with first mate Andy (his real name is John), Chrysa leaned romantically over the rail, her mermaidlike curls tangling in the salty breeze, her faery-sweet features turning the palest chartreuse as the waters reached up to embrace her. Connie G., on the other hand, had managed to wrap herself up like an Eskimo, avoiding any and all wave contact; Joanna had found a position of comfort, leaning up against the cabin; and Annelize, being Dutch, stood straight as a totem pole—calm, reserved and unruffled.

"We were rockin' and rollin' up in the back," says Ann. Ann, though most people wouldn't guess it, is a bit of a cowgirl. She's an expert on guns and has a heavy foot on the SUV accelerator; I learned this when she accompanied me on a rainforest assignment. "The captain's buddy was watching us to make sure we didn't fall in," she continued. "God, it was invigorating."

I imagine Ann bracing herself for the wild ups and downs and loving it: the bronco-busting American, the gal on the mechanical bull. According to Ann, Mary Jean, our incipient tri-athlete, was using the experience to practice pilates. When we'd rocket through a tough patch, she'd hiss in warning, "Try to protect your core."

In thirteen-foot seas with a southeasterly wind force of five to six knots, we ran to Roches Point at the mouth of the harbor and then to Power Head scanning the gray-green seas for a spyhop, a breach, a loptail—any sign at all of cetaceans, any momentary flash of a whale. The high seas were relentless, the horizon unbroken. It wasn't long before our group began to hallucinate sea life.

"Look over there, a pod of dolphins!"

"Yes! Yes! I see them."

"So do I."

Not really. There were no dolphins, but I didn't care. Like Ann, I was having the time of my life, loving it as we punched through a wave or crested it, hanging for a moment before crashing down into the trough. It was awesome, a bone-and-organ-jarring hurtle over the bounding main. No wonder our tour operators posted a warning to pregnant women and people with back problems on their website.

Mike, I came to learn, is a member of the Royal National Lifeboat Institution, which is similar to our United States Coast Guard. In a power boat training course, he had learned to navigate without sight; they had to "feel" the seas.

"They trained us by blindfolding us," he said.

I closed my eyes for a moment as the craft pitched and rolled, imagined piloting it in a blindfold, pictured myself smashing the boat into a cruise ship.

"Cool," I said, opening my eyes in a new kind of awe, sitting next to the curl-surfing ninja.

The swells rose in height and the winds pummeled the cabin. Those on deck popped inside, some wet as water spaniels, hair lank and drippy, mugs glistening with salt spume. Mike judged it wise to head back to the harbor and did so with amazing velocity. On the seven-ton Mischief we skated the high seas, running past the fortresses of Camden, Carlisle and Fort Mitchell and on toward Cobh, situated on the largest island in the lower harbor, where the big cruise ships berth. He then ran off past Monkstown and Passage West on the western shore and into Lake Mahon and Blackrock where we moored ever so briefly, stopping in at a pub for a heart- and hand-warming Irish whiskey and a pint. From Blackrock we headed to Cork City in the upper harbor. On the return we ran behind Haulbowline Island, which the Irish Navy—only eight ships on this day (and any day)—calls home. By the time we ran past Spike Island our spirits were serene, the water and wind and exhilaration having worked their inevitable magic. Much too soon we were back at Crosshaven, gathering our sodden affairs and bidding reluctant farewells.

We did not see a single fish that day. Not a seal or a dolphin, much less a whale. I can't remember if we saw many birds either, be they petrel or shearwater or fulmar or gull . . . well, maybe some gulls; yet I think we all had a fabulous time.

We ended the day anchored in chairs in perhaps the finest restaurant of the trip: elegant Finders Inn Restaurant in Nohaval, where the candlelight danced on the brick and old wood as we supped on delicious course after course of fresh fish, roast duck, perfectly grilled meats and an amazing assortment of potatoes. We toasted our travels, waxed nostalgic under the influence of excellent wines, and grew sleepy after all the excitement. The world, as I recall, was rocking for me when we left the restaurant, but certainly not from rough seas.

Changing Tides

ANNELIZE GOEDBLOED

The sailing boats lean over in the shiny mud of Cork Harbor, indecently turning up their bottoms. Various gulls and waders trample around. Soon we turn inland. The tangy smell of kelp lying like spit on the fringes of the shore disappears as we dive into the trenches of the country roads of southern County Cork. My hands can almost touch the bells of the fuchsia and pick up the perfume of the honeysuckle that are an integral part of the hedges.

Our cab driver, yet another Irish Mike, slightly pregnant and jolly, speeds along, talking profusely into his cell phone in his Irish tongue, which I only half understand. I nearly have a heart attack every time we meet a car; it is really difficult to adjust to the left-side driving here, and his one-handed approach to the wheel doesn't help.

I sit back and muse. So much is familiar, yet so much more has changed since I, a native of Holland, first visited Ireland in 1960.

The land is still green. Mike says it is "over-green" this year. A mosaic of all shades of green over soft, undulating hills. Meadows, wheat, corn, potatoes, ferns, woods. It is a tranquil landscape that goes on and on. The grass is not greener over the next hill; here it is all green. Coming from an overcrowded country, as I do, a horizon without a human artifact always gives a sensation of relief: like coming out of a party into fresh air.

I know I shouldn't be fooled, because every inch of this land has been worked and exploited. This green of Ireland is like the green sheet over a surgery patient. It covers the hard history of Ireland. Images of the emaciated faces of the people during the Great Famine in the mid-nineteenth century intrude upon the peacefully grazing cows.

Under centuries of British rule, Ireland was a nation of paupers and beggars. Then during the Great Famine, caused by the loss of the bountiful potato crops that had fed them for generations, the Irish starved. The population was halved by death from starvation and emigration, falling from eight million to four million. In the seaside town of Cobh, I visit the Cobh Heritage Centre which vividly shows the whole story. I leave with the same silenced awe I experienced at the Jewish memorial in Jerusalem.

I focus on the arrangement of the fields when we drive along—whenever a gap in the hedges enables a view. Meadows are predominant. Where are the familiar black mounds in them that pockmark our meadows in Holland? Are there no moles in Ireland? Mike confirms that when I question him. It is hard to imagine how poor Catholic tenant farmers ever squeezed a living out of less than a few acres here. Now dairy farms milking a few hundred cows have taken over.

And where are those cute thatched roofed cottages I remember? There were chickens scurrying on the dirt floor, a pig peeking in, and sods of turf warming me along with the beaker of home-brewed poteen, the local whiskey, in those cottages where long ago I was welcomed with such incredible hospitality. That past has been swept away into renovation provided with European Community funds, I am told. Now there are simple, dull, square boxes dotting the countryside. I find nothing charming in the looks of the silage with the car tires stacked against the black plastic, nor the prefab-barns and milking parlors.

I have to ask myself, too, how often as wealthy travelers we like the picturesque scenes of poverty. Even acknowledging that, I still miss seeing chickens and pigs outside some farm anywhere in County Cork now. Yet the land looks well-tended and neat with age-old, bark-clad trees still standing on guard.

Then an intriguing question occurs to me.

"How about leprechauns?" I ask our Mike when he takes a breath in between his cell phone chats. They are the ones who always appealed to me, if only because they smoke and drink like me. "Are they day or night people?"

That particular aspect of their character is not described in what I have read about them. Mike believes that as an Irishman—or perhaps just as a man in general—he should have an answer to everything.

"Definitely night people," he responds.

"This means that they sleep during the day?"

Mike confirms it off-handedly. He thinks I am crazy asking these questions. I decide I should learn more about faeries: they always go to bed at sunrise after a night of mischief and that would also suit my rhythm.

We pass small towns with sweet names such as Ballydehob, Skibbereen, Carrigaline or Ringaskiddy, now the site of a Pfizer factory. Mike proudly points his red-haired finger at the plant that produces the world supply of Viagra. His demeanour assures that he doesn't need that. Yet? I don't ask. But it is just one sign that industry now dominates once-rural Ireland. The electronic business is flourishing. Building activity is seen everywhere. The economy is booming, creating jobs, and descendants of emigrants come back again to work, boosting pride. The Celtic Tiger is blowing flames, and now far surpasses the English economy—another boon to the Irish ego. There are jobs and space enough. Even immigration is embraced, especially of Poles, who also revitalize the Catholic Church with its fading attendance.

The land, capped by magisterial clouds, feels vast and empty. Once Ireland was covered with woods, but now just patches remain. Deforestation from ship building in the Middle Ages is said to be the main cause. Not all problems can be blamed on modern life. Recent reforestation with improbable trees like pine and spruce has increased the amount of woodlands to only thirteen percent, but that is up from six percent. I don't see any wildlife in this land, no rabbit, hare, or pheasant. They should be here, and so should deer and wild boar. Didn't the old Druids once hunt them in their woodland habitat and cook them for ceremonial feasts?

A single cloud decides to take a leak. A few hundred meters further it is dry. Mike manoeuvres our cab through the narrow streets of Clonakilty, one of those small towns with an abundant history but a rather non-descript present, except for the always wonderfully adorned pubs flashing signs for Beamish or Murphy's. I see only few typical Irish red heads, and the locals are wearing T-shirts, slippers, and shorts, showing hairy legs, since it is supposed to be summer. In the cab the heater is on.

Pointed church spires rise above Clonakilty in English gothic style. One Catholic, the other Protestant. Both parishes now live in peace next to each other. The Celtic Tiger has conquered the intense hatred, gnawed the smirk off the haughtiness of the British, but history is not forgotten. Reminders are seen in the statues of heroes fighting for Irish independence and memorials to honor patriots in almost every village and town.

Gliding by in our cab, everything is very quiet. Mike's favorite CD with Irish folk music whines on and on. A car coming from the opposite direction, materializing around a bend in the meandering road, is sure to startle me. Unfortunately, left-side driving continues. I can understand the difficulty in changing that ridiculous British inheritance, but it is bad for my health when speeding along the narrow, walled, country roads. Mike doesn't mind of course. He proudly points his red-haired finger at another hero at a crossroad.

We circle Cork Harbor, one of the largest natural harbors in the world. Several charming villages are dotted around it. Stacks of lobsterpots rest on the quay. A few big fishing boats and a herd of small ones stretch their lines against the current. The entire coast of Ireland is protected by the Irish Navy that consists of eight ships and some fourteen hundred enlisted seamen. I imagine that apart from the occasional excitement of bringing in a foreign fishing trawler intruding the international waters, life in this navy is comfortable. It is a good indication of the peace that has come over this western-most island of Europe, a peace that has been so much fought for.

To my delight, Ireland's biggest whiskey factory happens to be in County Cork, in Midleton, producing the best known brands: Paddy, Jameson (pronounced Jemmison), and Tullamore Dew. To Mike's distress, a heavy tax of fifty percent on these delights inhibits profuse enjoyment. Looking at the fleshy waves where the padding of his tummy is spreading, I believe he might be actually saved by the government of Ireland.

Mike explains, "Irish WhiskEY is distilled three times, Scots whiskY only once."

We swerve along the dented coastline. Everywhere tongues of sea are lapping into the flesh of the land. A strong wind flops up white crests on the waves. I imagine the folk bending against the wind on these lonely roads bearing heavy blocks of butter on their backs, travelling night and day, on their way to the Cork Butter Exchange. The salted butter was exported to all parts of the world. The Butter Road and its contribution to the development of Ireland's commerce and communities has slipped into the past. The railway and local creameries finished it off long ago.

The villages up against the coastal hills of southern County Cork show rows of colored houses like those in a game of monopoly, all hugging bunches of hortensia. There are no city regulations on the colors, so homeowners are left to their own aesthetic devices. The results are often so appalling they are charming.

The sailboats are bobbing in Cork Harbor. It is high tide. The tide will go out again.

Like the tide, the Irish economy may slow down. Too many foreign laborers may cause resentment. New wealth is not easy to handle. But the resilient Irish will find a way to adapt to their new role as a strong nation at peace.

KATHLEEN,
tHE DAUGHTER OF HOULAHAN

⧖

With dreams burned out like cinders
and spirits crushed like chalk,
the royal men of Ireland,
deprived of country, stalk
the palace courts and halls of foreign France and Spain
or, on some foreign strand,
beneath a foreign reign
fight foreign nation's causes since forbad to fight their own.
But fast the day is coming
when the tyrant British Crown,
from every Irish acre and every Irish town,
will be driven out in warring
by the Royal Warrior Son
           of *Kathleen, the Daughter of Houlahan.*

It will not now be long before the nation ring
a million bells of freedom
and a million throats will sing
and harp the many songs that are so long unsung—
throats so long struck dumb
singing in their native tongue.
Our exiled men returned, like birds in early spring,
among their kith and kin,
will also toast and sing
the ancient lays of Ireland and the freedom newly won
by him, our new born Finn,
the Royal Warrior Son
        of *Kathleen, the Daughter of Houlahan.*

How many generations in every Irish home
have prayed that foreign nations
would in their warships come;
their thousand masts a forest against an Irish sky,
their guns no imitations,
their steel pikes eight feet high;
would come to free our country, a hundred thousand strong?
Our scholars look like scarecrows,
our poets sing no song;
with prices on their heads, our priests are on the run.
But our answer to our foes
is the Royal Warrior Son
        of *Kathleen, the Daughter of Houlahan.*

The hair of Princess Kathleen is gold as autumn grain,
and all her gold-ring curls
fall like a gold-leaf train;
her eyes are sapphire lakes in mists of morning sun,
a gown of purple furls
a form of gods alone.
Her voice is pure as silver, with all the silver tone
of a love song on a hill
when the piper pipes alone.
To guard the ageless beauty is what has to be done
led by the warring skill
of the Royal Warrior Son
            of *Kathleen, the Daughter of Houlahan.*

These tyrants who suppress us and think our spirit spent
will soon see justice done.
Soldiers will be sent
from friendly kings in Europe to help us in our need.
Good Virgin, ask your Son—
who led His chosen seed
of Israel free—to guide and give us courage
all through the battle hour.
And may He too encourage,
both young and old alike, to fight until we've won
his rightful kingdom for
the Royal Warrior Son
            of *Kathleen, the Daughter of Houlahan.*

The Signs:

Our priests and our nuns in unison pray.
The bones of our dead not quietly away.
The sun is the face of a furnace fire
and the light of the moon is a tune on a lyre.
The heavens are covered with hammered gold
and the stars have increased a hundred fold.
All signs that freedom will soon be won
by none but the Royal Warrior Son
of *Kathleen, the Daughter of Houlahan.*

—DESMOND O'GRADY

A Moving Benedict-ion

Connie Burke

olf is part of Ireland's psyche. It is a game of tradition and ritual with tendencies towards the tragicomic, giving the player insight into the historical character of Ireland and the very temperament of its most humble citizens. The Irish are passionate about the game. Like a rare *Connemara* (Irish malted whiskey), it has character, a slow and sweet warming comfort, and a long peaty finish that lingers long after it has gone. One only craves for more.

In Ireland, golf is a way of life. You walk. You slowly move across a terrain on foot—connecting to it with the senses and awareness; evaluating, deciding, accepting outcomes, weighing up new situations. You learn that golf is a game of going along, not going ahead.

"Like life, golf is unpredictable," Benedict, my Irish golf

buddy, said as he closed the boot of his car and handed me a timeworn set of borrowed clubs. "You learn to overcome the smaller inconsistencies, the smaller mistakes we make from one game to the next or from one hole to the other."

Walking towards the clubhouse of Monkstown Golf Club, County Cork, the wind bore a dog's bark from the hillside beyond as the grey sky slowly rolled back like an eyelid leaving us under a vast blue stare. In the distance the countryside was speckled with friesian cows and sheep with cork-screw fleece grazing above those dark brown cliffs that hug the restless Atlantic.

"Clear skies!" I said in disbelief. "Think we'll beat the rain today?" I asked while watching the dark clouds move away from us. The chirping of birds was so constant it was not so much sound as a condition of the Irish parkland course.

"With a bit o'luck, we can get in eighteen," Benedict said with a slight grin on his face. One should never forecast a full day of clear skies in Ireland. Even in the midst of a warm summer.

Monkstown (*Baile an Mhanaigh* in Irish) is conveniently situated just ten minutes by car from both Cork and the old garrison town of Cobh (pronounced cove), formerly Queenstown. Its name derives from a parish town in the barony of Kerrycurrihy, County Cork where a small establishment of Benedictine monks called Legan Abbey, belonging to the priory of St. John's, Waterford, was formed in the fourteenth century.

Monkstown Golf Club rejoices in its distinguished history. From the seventh tee-box the players behold the ruins of the old Castle which provided members with a distinctive clubhouse before the ravages of time made the grand old building uninhabitable. The shell that remains is a poignant reminder of past glories.

Originally called Monkstown Castle, it was an Elizabethan styled home built on the side of a glen in 1636 by Eustace Gould. In 1639, the once-proud building that enhanced such a glorious and significant site was rebuilt by John and Anastasia Archdeacon.

"The castle cost only a few pennies to build due to the business acumen of Anastasia." Benedict remarked. "While her husband fought in the army of the King of Spain, she deducted the cost of food from the workmen's wages and paid very little for the building."

During the changes in the political situation in England in the seventeenth century, with the conflict between Monarchy and Parliamentarians led by Oliver Cromwell, the Castle passed through different hands before going to the Boyle Family. The DeVesci and Longford families inherited the property through marriage and the last owner, De Vesci, sold the property to Monkstown Golf Club in 1959 for four thousand pounds. It is fitting that the outline of the ruined castle forms the crest of its club.

"Founded in 1908, Monkstown is one of the four original golf courses of County Cork," Benedict recollected as trolleys were brought out to us from the pro shop. The other three are Cork Golf Club (1888), Muskerry (1907) and Douglas (1909). Since then, many more have developed in the area, notably Fota Island, Harbour Point and Lee Valley. Almost every town on the Emerald Isle has its own golf course: four hundred in a country of just over four million people.

"The first Golfing Union was the Golfing Union of Ireland, in 1891," he proudly added. "Your USGA was founded in 1894."

"Where are the Scots in all this?" I inquired, curious to hear an Irish response. "Don't they claim to be the first to play golf?"

"Who knows?" Benedict shrugged. "The Dutch say they played it first around the dunes of Holland. But the Scots say they were the first to put holes in the ground!"

Monkstown is an inland course set amongst native oak, pine, ash, cedar, hazel and beech trees, to name a few. Looking at early photographs hanging in the new clubhouse, the course showed mature beech and pine trees that were most probably part of Monkstown Castle. Today, some of the new fairways are framed with firs and pine. According to James Healy, a consultant agronomist, such was the "fashion adopted in the middle of the last century because of the speed at which they grew and undoubtedly because of their economic purchase cost." The golf club is fortunate to have within its membership plant lovers and experts. Native indigenous trees were planted and the fairways were framed with a mixture of grey willows and poplars.

Walking over to the first hole, I set my borrowed clubs down next to the ladies first tee. Looking into the golf bag for the appropriate club choice for this hole, a par three at 171 meters, I balked at the paucity of clubs.

"There are only eight clubs in this bag," I announced. I was not only missing a wedge, eight, six, four, and three iron, but my only wood was an unmarked thirty-year-old, steel-shafted club with a head the size of an egg. I was definitely going to have to negotiate the unpredictable during this round of golf.

"Let's have a friendly competition," Benedict proposed.

"Why not," replied Annelize, our Dutch playing partner.

Benedict is competitive. He claims that his competitiveness has improved his quality of life.

"Competition is healthy if it is done in the right spirit," he said. "Lose your competitive edge and you lose your outlook on life."

He teed up his ball. "The first hole is tricky, ladies," he said while taking a practice swing with a mid-range wood.

"But don't fret," he continued. "A four is quite acceptable here."

He sensed my dismay.

Golf can be ever so frustrating when you don't have your own clubs. Annelize and I were prepared to blame the unfamiliarity of the course and the lack of club choice for a poor score. We reminded each other that we were there for the "walk".

"Wish I had my Big Bertha," I murmured to myself. "Need to drive my ball!"

New golf technology undoubtedly brings new powers and awareness into play for those of us who pursue the game with passion. Theories involving the simultaneity of past and future abound. Our obsession with projectiles is in our DNA. Our urge to see our ball flying high and far derives from our Paleolithic past, from the hunt. We love to see the spear or stone or javelin in flight. We love the anticipation. The sight of our golf balls hanging in space anticipates our desire for transcendence. But staring at the "egghead" at my feet was disillusioning. I quickly forgot about the freedom of flight and decided to use a club that would ensure some gravity at impact.

Annelize sensed my despair.

"Try this," she said, handing me a Calloway rescuer she found in her bag, the only wood she possessed.

"Nothing to lose," she simpered.

I teed up the ball wondering if it was too low and I might miss altogether, so I walked away, smiled at my playing partners, and returned to tee up higher. I let my hands fall into place on the rubber grip. Going over my personal checklist, I dwelled on pivot, shoulder, weight transference, hip turn, wrist release, timing, and, of course keeping my head down.

I took in a few deep breaths, smelling the heather and freshly cut grass of the fairways fringed with laurel, holly, and cotoneaster. I quieted all those inner conversations so prevalent in the game of golf and surrendered to the moment.

"Here goes," I whispered. Arm socket and neck jerked as the rescuer met little resistance. I looked up to see the trajectory of my ball rising near-vertically and heading straight to the green.

"Lucky shot," I said, breathing a long sigh of relief as the ball hit the front fringe of the green and slowly rolled just left of the pin.

"You're in the stitch!" shouted Benedict. "Might be a 'gimme'!"

It wasn't a "gimme" and with a five-pound-steel-toothed putter as old as the course, I was relieved to make par.

Playing on, we experienced the highs and lows that go with any golf game. We all had shots that led to feelings of great accomplishment and, unfortunately, feelings of hopelessness and despair. Hole after hole, the beauty of the Irish landscape overwhelmed any negative emotion the game could induce.

The third hole (par five) brought us to the plateau of the course with magnificent views of Cork's inner harbor, overlooking the River Lee, and the islands of Haulbowline and Spike.

The scenery was breathtaking. We were breathless. We pulled our trolleys uphill on a very long and tough par five, fifth hole.

"We call this hole 'coronary hill'," Benedict grimaced. "Yet I have not heard of any tragedies there except a double bogey or worse!"

The round with Benedict and Annelize confirmed everything I heard and read about golf in Ireland. Though he didn't tell us until the fifth hole that Monkstown was sometimes referred to as "Bunkerstown," we managed to stay out of the sand most of the round.

Things quieted down around the seventh and eighth holes as we skirted around the ruins of the old castle, reflecting upon the history of the area and that of Anglo-Ireland. Benedict broke the ghostly silence and reminded us that "the old oak trees make life difficult with any wayward shot."

Crossing the road to the newer part of the course, the match was pretty even. Playing skins, our counts fluctuated like our good and bad drives. The bunkers became less intimidating as our balls were more often drawn towards the many stately old trees that defined the fairways and enriched the sylvan setting. Sculpted into the landscape along with oak and pine were mountain ash, whitebeam, blue cedar and even a few trees from the southern hemisphere, eucalyptus. The popularity of coniferous planting in the 1960s had even introduced broad-reaching varieties of cypress. As wonderful as the trees were, they were most definitely a reason to proceed with a degree of caution.

The fifteenth and sixteenth holes have fabulous new water features. A visual highlight, the sixteenth Augusta-style hole, looks improbably perfect, all lush green and blue, and banked by a colorful array of annuals. The club claims that those holes provide a nice contrasting challenge and help to complete a lay-out that demanded subtlety and courage in equal measure.

Benedict reminded us that the fifteenth and sixteenth holes "demand the use of every club in the ol'golf bag." Surely he wasn't trying to humor us.

By the time we reached the eighteenth hole, we had company. Rain. Leaves reeled down upon our rain-soaked heads. Fringes of grass waved goodbye to us as we squelched along. Annelize and I had the majority of skins. Benedict would have to win the next two holes to claim victory.

"It's well burst now, i'nt it?" Benedict shouts. The dark clouds wove a silent dance for their native son. "It all comes down to the last hole, dear ladies," he yowled, drawing out every syllable like a Gaelic bard.

The Irish live with bad weather. And winning brings out the best in an Irish gent. Benedict exemplifies Celtic nature: he believes fanatically, trusts implicitly, hopes infinitely, and, perhaps, revenges implacably. These qualities make the Celt the great motive force of the world, ever striving against limitations towards some vision of ideal splendor. Benedict needed to win. No different than Padraig, the pride of Irish golf, who survived a calamitous finish in regulation and a hair-raising bogey putt in the 2007 playoff to bring the "Championship" trophy home to Ireland.

Standing in puddles on a rain-drenched eighteenth green, Annelize and I winced as we watched our victory wash away with three putts each. We laughed. We loved it all. It was, after all, only befitting that our very own Benedict take the win in Monkstown!

A Pub Story

Ann Kathleen Ure

When we stepped inside the Pine Lodge, our senses were overwhelmed by the musky sea of testosterone. During the day the cozy Myrtleville pub in County Cork looked out over the expansive Atlantic Ocean, but at night it was a shoulder-to-shoulder man-magnet with all the energy directed towards its small, polished bar. The fragrance of local Murphy's and Beamish stouts greeted us, too. The fumes from the beers formed a pungent cocktail when mixed with the men's cologne and sweat. It was a snootful of a first impression.

The gang of twenty to thirty men parted when we writers, Linda, Chrysa and I, entered. Their pints led their hands in an automatic toast or greeting—so many and so close that we could almost taste the rich, bitter brews ourselves. It was ten in the evening on a Monday night and we had just completed a

223

late stroll around the neighborhood. A block earlier we'd met up with a man who advised that another of the writers was "holding court" at the Pine Lodge and might need an escort back to our B&B up the road.

I felt one fellow's arm on mine and I turned to him to ask the question that had brought us into the pub.

"Where's Doreen?"

"Ah, Doreen," he replied, extending the ee's with a slow purr that was loud enough to entertain the crowd of men around him. "She's just left."

"Alone?" I asked.

"Yes," he replied with a grin, "but not for our lack of trying!"

The men were still thumping themselves on their backs for their good humor and company when we scooted out the back door. I had enjoyed this brief encounter, too, having read about the wit and camaraderie to be found in Irish pubs. In fact, one of the reasons I wanted to visit the Emerald Isle was to shoot the breeze with the locals I would encounter on the streets and in the pubs. My expectations had been set: ask for directions and expect a charming fifteen-minute interrogation into your background before being personally accompanied to your destination; slip onto a bar stool for a pint and leave hours later, soused at closing—with twenty new best friends. This was going to be terrific!

The pub scene portion of my travel plan didn't pan out as I had envisioned, but—as the guy in the bar had said—it wasn't for my lack of trying. It was just two nights later that I returned, with Doreen, to the Pine Lodge, anticipating the best. We found the mood to be relatively quiet and the crowd an even mix of men and women with a few kids in tow. Perhaps it was too early in the evening and things would liven up once the children were put to bed, I thought. We'll just give it some time.

But the magic never really came to pass. For the next two hours I sat at a small round table with a semi-scruffy threesome named Mick, Robbie and Jimmy. They looked to be in their forties. Mick could have passed for a San Francisco hippie from the 1960s, magically transported to the tiny hamlet of Myrtleville. Jimmy was a family man out for a Friday night while the family was away. He had that bit of desperation about him that said: let's make the most of tonight, lads, cause the wife and kids will be back tomorrow. Robbie, who sat closest to me, was the most laid back. He sported the buzz cut that was popular all over Ireland either due to fashion, the "glorious summer weather" (declared without a hint of irony though it capped at a high of sixty-three degrees Fahrenheit during our stay), or an attempt to stave off the appearance of thinning hair.

I thought I could sit back with a Beamish in one hand and a pen in the other and be regaled by their stories, jotting down the juiciest tidbits. Unfortunately, they immediately hushed themselves silent when I announced that I was writing about pubs and their patrons. It took another round of pints—they drank Guinness and Murphy's—for their tongues to loosen. When they did, the sounds they made were all but intelligible. I found that Mick and Robbie put a bit of effort into enunciating when they spoke to me. But when Jimmie relayed an anecdote I was hard-pressed to comprehend one out of every five words. It crossed my mind that they might be intentionally mining their vernacular and accents to inhibit my ability to record any specific stories. But, more likely they were just enjoying gabbing at a fast clip with their equally fast friends. At one point when Robbie knew I was struggling to keep up with one of his stories, he leaned over and asked

"Did you catch any of that last one, lass?" I shook my head no.

"Well," he said, "I'm going to tell it to you again and this time I'll say it s-l-o-w."

"I was telling the lads about my brother Michael who has a bit of a problem with the drink," Robbie began. "Michael told me that he went on a terrible bender and woke up in a strange place. He was still so drunk the next morning that he couldn't even remember his own name."

"Well," Robbie continued, "he said that the only way his name would come back to him was to sing to himself: 'Happy birthday to you, happy birthday to you. Happy birthday, dear Michael; happy birthday to you.'"

As I had already downed two pints and lowered my expectations for the evening, I rewarded Robbie's tale with a small guffaw. But I simultaneously realized two things: that the story had been just as charming in its unintelligible, Irish-accented version, and that this particular night in this particular pub with these particular gentlemen was not going to fuel an essay on the boundless wit and wisdom of the Irish. I went back to our B&B with my blank notebook and a headache soon thereafter.

Over the ensuring week, my subsequent visits to pubs were no more fruitful. The sauciest conversations I had were with my fellow travelers. There was that time that an older gentleman at the Armada in Kinsale started to chat me up, but then his buddy called him off by announcing that his wife was looking for him. A brief foray into another local pub was no more successful. The few men there were all glued to the television screen watching a football match. They didn't look up when we arrived or when we departed.

I also discovered that the wait staff didn't necessarily care to coddle the tourist. The look I got when I asked for a decaffeinated Irish coffee was humbling. In fact it pushed me into ordering pints, nothing but pints, for the rest of my stay. This strategy kept me safe from further pub faux pas—like asking for a Guinness lite on tap.

Intent on keeping alive the quest for pub camaraderie, I cajoled friends Mary Jean and Gail into accompanying me to the historic and funky Hi-B pub in Cork City. It was tiny and charming, but utterly devoid of funk that day. Twenty or so patrons hunched over their pints barely speaking to one another, much less to us. Even the waitress behind the bar failed to give us a shout-out during the entire fifteen minutes one of us stood and two of us perched on folding chairs near one of the pub's few tables. Located above a wig shop, this day the Hi-B smelled equally of Irish stout and the chemicals used in styling wigs. With no clear signs of conviviality, and slightly intoxicated by the fumes, we moved on.

They say the best time to find something is when you stop looking for it. Towards the end of our trip, in spite of my heavy financial and caloric investments in new friends Beamish, Murphy's, and dear Guinness, I was close to conceding that my love tryst with the patrons and pubs of County Cork was not to be consummated. On our last evening we writers ventured to Crosshaven for a bite and an evening of music. After a delicious bowl of seafood chowder and two chunks of brown bread, I was tempted to call it a night. But with the urging of my travel mates, I powered on to one last pub. The effort paid off.

The pub was Buckley's on Lower Road. Most of our group settled themselves around a circular table towards the rear of the establishment. I plopped myself down at the bar with Mary Jean and Gail. We were adjacent to the area where a small band began to assemble. We were also within earshot of the proprietor behind the bar, Nina Casey.

Nina was the antidote to my pub slump. She elevated my evening from half-pints of Beamish to shots of Bushmills Black Bush Special Irish Whiskey. She listened. She called me darlin'. And, as she served alongside her sister, Ronnie, she explained how Ireland's pubs, especially those without kitchens (hence no food service) were struggling to survive.

"Pubs run in my family," Nina said. "My parents owned Coughlin's in Kinsale before they bought Buckley's. Now my husband Pat and I own and run Buckley's."

Nina continued, saying "as recently as fifteen years ago

we'd be busy all afternoon with men conducting business here. They'd sell their livestock over a pint. They'd drink; they'd share news and stories; they'd strike up deals. Sometimes they'd dispute the same deals the next day because they'd been too drunk to negotiate fairly."

She went on to tell me that business wasn't done that way anymore, that people don't have the time to sit in a pub during the work day, and that there is a greater emphasis and enforcement of drinking and driving laws.

When I asked if there were still pubs known for their relaxed, convivial clientele that swapped stories for hours, she said "yes." But she also said that they were usually older pubs—fraying about the edges and tucked away off the main streets—and that their clientele was largely the retired men who were nostalgic for days gone by.

As my trip was nearing its end, I regretted that I wouldn't have more time to explore County Cork's throw-back pubs to hang out with the old guard. But the moment of reflection was brief. I put down my pen and took in the scene that was unfolding around me. Bottles, pitchers and pints clanked as they were passed back and forth over the bar. The music, previously tame, was pulsating as was the crowd that now gathered around the musicians. The small talented band was dominating the mood and intensifying the collective energy. Feet tapped. Knuckles rapped. Fists pounded. It had gotten steamy in Buckley's, and the sticky-sweet aromas of sweat and ale filled the air.

The musicians were swapping turns singing. Most of the

pieces were traditional and upbeat but some were tender, even mournful. By the time they got around to an Irish classic, "The Dawning of the Day," I was all ears. The rest of our group had moved up front, too. Everyone wanted to be closer to these artists who had brought Ireland to life for us with their music.

An announcement that a group of writers, most from California, were in the crowd drew a cheer. It also prompted the band to mix it up with their song choices. Soon we were enjoying an even wider range of tunes including popular selections like Sting's "Fields of Gold" and the "Tennessee Waltz." A true Irish tenor stepped out of nowhere and serenaded the room with a romantic ballad. The crowd went wild.

Inhibitions diminished in direct proportion to pints consumed as others took a turn at the microphone. Gail joined the band for a folk song. We had fallen under the spell of the music, the ambiance, and one another. I felt a surge of pub-love for this big, tipsy, happy and, alternately, weepy-eyed family of friends.

Then, all too quickly, the lights dipped to signal the approach of closing time. A last round of drinks was quickly dispensed, and the band played on—a little more frenzied if that was possible. No one wanted to leave. But when we did, it was one hell of an exit.

The band's final song brought everyone to their feet. It was an over-the-top number that let us squeeze out every last ounce of emotion. I crooned loudly and gesticulated to all my new friends. The crowd edged towards the door but didn't push past it. It was a Harry Nilsson tune from the seventies that the band

had chosen to shut it down.
   Together we sang:

> *No, I can't forget this evening*
> *Or your face as you were leaving*
> *But I guess that's just the way the story goes*
> *You always smile but in your eyes your sorrow*
> *shows*
> *Yes, it shows*
>
> *No, I can't forget tomorrow*
> *When I think of all my sorrows*
> *When I had you there but then I let you go*
> *And now it's only fair that I should let you know*
> *What you should know*
>
> *I can't live if living is without you*
> *I can't live, I can't give anymore*
> *I can't live if living is without you*
> *Can't live, I can't give anymore . . . .*

   That night I dreamt about our experience at Buckley's. Two days later I was en route for California, replaying the entire evening's events and Nilsson's "Without You" lyrics in my head. It hadn't been the pub experience I went looking for. It was better.

CELTIC TIGER, PRAIRIE DOG

GAIL STRICKLAND

he musicians of *Na Ciaroga* (the Beatles) trickled into Buckley's pub in Crosshaven. Tom Kilcummin brought his guitar, Robert Foster his banjo, Lucy Cullinane her fiddle, Jimmy Delaney his button accordion and *bodhran* (an Irish hand drum pronounced 'bow rahn') and . . . what was that?

"*Uilleann* pipes," Richard O'Farrell answered and immediately brought them over to show me.

"What?"

"*Uilleann* pipes."

I was surprised that this strong, gentle giant of a man was so willing to stop setting up his pipes just to answer my question. He even spelled the pipes' name twice for me. They looked a little like a big brother to the bagpipes, except there was no reed, no place to blow: all the air was produced by pumping a

233

bellows beneath the arm and playing notes through chanters. Richard is reputedly one of the best pipers in all of southern Ireland. That was easy to believe once I heard him play.

I looked around the dark room filled with smiles and tapping feet. The walls were covered with paintings of sailing vessels, the shelves lined with beer steins of the world. There was a constant stream of mostly men going back and forth to the bar where Nina, the owner, smoothly poured a tall one with a careful nod to listen. She was dressed in a pin-striped blouse and had a trim figure and short gray hair. Her face seemed pleased and proud to be sharing her pub with her community.

Marguerite and John Cullinane, the fiddle player's parents, came and sat down next to me. Their daughter Lucy, with dark hair pulled back from her sweet face, focused completely on the notes that leapt from her bow. Two small, round tables in front of the musicians were littered with pints of beer, lemonade for Lucy, and bones. Bones? I stared at two bones lying in front of the drummer, wedged between a full and empty pint, and wondered if they were deer bones. It reminded me of W.B.Yeats's poem, "Dreaming of the Bones."

> *Have not old writers said*
> *That dizzy dreams can spring*
> *From the dry bones of the dead?*

Thinking of Yeats, I remembered that a French priest lost the poet's bones. The tour guides like to tell visitors that he is buried beneath Ben Bulben in his beloved Sligo, Ireland, but that's not the whole story. Yeats died in Roquebrune in southern France in 1939. His wife intended for the grave in the churchyard to be only temporary, but World War II intervened. Due to a clerical error and the priest's confusion about the poet's identity, his grave was dug up and his bones were removed to an ossuary, a graveyard for unidentified corpses, where skulls and limbs were stored separately. When Yeats' wife returned at the end of the war and demanded her husband's remains, the church searched the ossuary and claimed to have found Yeats's remains. They were returned to Ireland in a coffin draped with an Irish flag and accompanied by a French honor guard. He was finally buried with all due pomp in 1948 in Drumcliff churchyard. Or so they say.

I sat back and closed my eyes and let the music carry me along. Lucy watched the other musicians with an intensity only matched by the pipe player, as he tucked the bellows beneath his massive left arm and pumped away while his fingers flew across the holes on the chanter. Jimmy played a wicked rhythm on the bones, and the banjo player's fingers flew across the strings. The musicians screamed for the sheer joy of it all.

It carried me back to my own roots, to the burrow, the Club 23 in Brisbane, California, where I played piano in an eclectic country-rock band called the Prairie Dogs. Bemused buffalo heads watched over the dance floor, while the crystal ball twirled, casting silver and red and blue over enthralled two-step dancers. I thought back to my first time on stage with "the dogs." I had trained for years in classical music, but improvising with a band was another world altogether.

"Take it, piano player," James, the guitar player had shouted to give me my turn to play my first improvised solo. I looked back at him with abject terror in my eyes. I could play Bach partitas and Beethoven sonatas, but me improvise? Where were those safe little black notes on the page that told me where the music was supposed to go next? Where was the composer to tell me what to do?

And what did I do that first time? I panicked. "No," I answered short and sweet.

Laughing at the memory, I opened my eyes to watch Lucy's bow fly across the strings of her fiddle, fierce and vibrant, transformed into a living beast, leaping and cavorting with the beat of the drum. The fire from her music was so wild, that it had shredded the horse hairs on her bow, so they waved at its tip like a soft mane. Listening to her play nothing but improvisation, I smiled to myself. Crosshaven or Brisbane, it doesn't matter where musicians gather, music transcends words. No wonder the Druid bards forbade anyone from writing down their songs. When I finally did break free from the intellectual approach of written music to experience the living heartbeat of improvisation, there was nothing else like it.

"You look utterly happy, Gail." Connie, our organizer, stopped by with a Beamish in her hand and a broad smile. She had arranged the music as a surprise for us.

I settled back in my chair and looked once more around the

room, realizing with a laugh that a new ritual had dawned on the Irish pub scene. Every so often, someone would reach in their pocket or purse and pull out their cell phone, open it to check for messages, his or her face briefly lit by the blue-green light. *"It's all here,"* I thought. *"Druid bards meet Celtic Tiger."* The Irish refer to the new Ireland, transformed by economic growth into a powerful contributor to the European Union, as the Celtic Tiger. The land of faeries and legend has enticed Johnson and Johnson, Price-Pfizer, and Pepsi, among other major companies, to establish their factories nestled between green fields. The cell phones seemed like an umbilical cord between the past and the future. It was a new ritual even for the cherub-faced bartender Noreen, who poured a pint for Ann and me before ending her shift. She then traded one side of the bar for the other as the musicians arrived. Accepting a pint offered by Nina, she perched on her stool as close to the musicians as she could. Though she seldom took her eyes off the musicians, every few songs she would pull her cell phone out of her pocket and peer into its eerie light to see if there was a call from her other world. A call from the Celtic Tiger? A reminder of jobs or family or ties to her modern life? All the Irish legends talk of people being snatched away to the land of the faeries, lost in the mists of time to a faery world that awakens at night. Perhaps the cell phone is her lifeline, her connection to a daytime life that keeps her safe and grounded to her modern reality. It would be easy to get swept away to faeryland by this music.

"Do you think traditions are being lost because of the Celtic

Tiger?" I asked Lucy's dad.

"No," he answered immediately, "Here it is, you see, in the music. I think it's stronger than ever. Changing. Growing. Now maybe the storytelling is about gone. Dead. Well, there be a few festivals. But the music is grand."

A local man stood up and started singing "The German Clock Winder." Lucy's father recognized the opening strands and suggested with a wry smile, "This is a very funny song. It has lots of connotations."

I thought back to the first time I heard a round table sharing of Irish musicians. We were at the Armada pub in Kinsale. I was already a huge fan of the Chieftains, and I thought I knew what to expect. I had not anticipated the joy, the boundless freedom and wordless communication between the players and their audience, the feeling of coming home. With a permanent smile plastered on my face, I danced in my seat, unable to sit still, wanting so much to play music with them. I looked around the pub at the others to see if they were as enthralled as I was.

A couple sat on one side of the pub, their backs against a deep red wall. The man was lanky, straight out of "American Gothic," a pint of Murphy's in his right hand instead of a pitchfork. He sat tall, eager, and leaned slightly forward in anticipation as the musicians cavorted through jigs and ballads around the table just in front of him. His wife sat beside her husband— shorter, rounder, softer, her smile a mere glimmer in pale blue eyes that darted glances between her husband's vigor and the galloping music.

I had a feeling that they were used to sitting always to the side, never center stage, never speaking out and being heard. But as the dark beer lowered in his glass, the man snatched up a metal bottle opener kept handy in his black trouser pocket and jigged a rhythm on the scarred wooden table. He cast a glance at me and smiled broadly, co-conspirators in table pounding. He'd taken up a rhythm, an offbeat canter to the drummer's own beat. The drummer heard us. I felt certain he did. He threw his head back, closed his eyes and stroked the goat skin with hand and stick to pattern the waves of guitar, banjo, flute and accordion that filled our gathering hall. The man's wife eased back on her padded bench, re-crossed her legs at the ankles, and smiled broadly at her husband. As she glanced as me, her smile thinned and diluted, then became irresistibly wide.

I was jolted from my musings back to Buckley's and realized the musicians had stopped playing. They turned as one to look at our group of writers.

"Can one of ye give us a song?" Tom Kilcummin, the guitarist, asked.

"Gail, you sing," my friends and fellow writers encouraged me.

"Go ahead, Gail." They turned to the waiting musicians. "She's a musician."

Tom's face lit up with new understanding and respect.

"But I played in Kinsale. It's someone else's turn."

Though I protested, I knew in my heart I really wanted to sing with these grand musicians. I wanted to blend my voice with theirs. I didn't want to say "no" one more time. Not again.

Never again.

"Oh, what do you play?" Tom asked, and I mimed playing piano.

"Would you like an instrument?" He immediately passed his beloved, hand-crafted guitar over the table covered with pints and lemonade and bones.

It didn't take me long to decide.

"It's in the key of D," I said. Almost all Irish songs are performed in the key of D and I guessed the *uilleann* pipes were probably tuned to D. "An old American folk song. Only three chords." I launched into,

> *Take this hammer, uh*
> *Carry to the Captain*
> *Take this hammer*
> *Carry to the Captain*

The musicians all joined in, a rousing wild cry of pipes and fiddle and accordion. I was in heaven. The Celtic Tiger danced with a Prairie Dog.

About the Contributors

ENISE ALTOBELLO, daughter of a butcher and a restaurant maven, granddaughter of a German gravedigger and a one-armed Cajun barbeque chef hails originally from the now famous Ninth Ward of New Orleans, just downriver from the French Quarter. Growing up among the graveyards of her Irish, German and African-American neighbors, she played hide-and-seek in the cities of the dead, learned to decipher the voodoo markings adorning the above-ground graves and honed her skills in palm reading, bar-hopping and fire baton twirling. Her achievements include the title of runner-up as Miss Majorette of Louisiana and a five-year reign as fancy strut champion for the National Baton Twirlers Association. In recent years, her greatest accomplishments have included working (for 3 days) as an itinerant goat milker and cooking paella in the back of a steamy truck in Provence. When she is not cooking, eating, drinking or gardening, she teaches English at an independent middle school in the Lower Garden District of New Orleans.

OANNA BIGGAR is a teacher, writer and traveler whose special places of the heart include the California coast and the South of France. She has a B.A. in Chinese and a Ph.D. in French literature. As a professional writer for twenty-five years, she has written poetry, fiction, personal essays, features, news and travel articles for hundreds of publications including *The Washington Post Magazine, Psychology Today, The International Herald Tribune* and *The Wall Street Journal.* Her book *Travels and Other Poems* was published in 1996, and her most recent travel essays have appeared in Sportsfanmagazine.com, *Floating through France: Life Between Locks on the Canal du Midi* and *Venturing in Southern Greece: the Vatika Odysseys*. She has taught journalism, creative writing, personal essay and travel writing at the Writer's Center in Bethesda, Maryland, since 1984 and "Spirit of Place" at the Writer's Center of Marin in San Rafael, California. In recent years she has also taught English, reading and writing at the University of the District of Columbia and at St. Martin de Porres Middle School in Oakland, California. (jobiggar@gmail.com)

ANDRA BRACKEN made the first of many journeys alone to Peru in 1976 where she walked the hills around Sacsayhuaman, photographed the stonework there and chartered a plane to fly over the lines at Nazca—all in the pursuit of art. More recently, with her husband, travels have been in pursuit of fish—fly fishing from the streams of Montana to the saltwater flats of the Seychelles. She is an artist by education and sensibility with a Masters in Fine Arts. Her sculpture has been exhibited in galleries and museums in the United States and is in private collections. Her chapbook of poems, *New Moon*, was published in 1999. She collaborated on *Meet Me at the Wayside Body Shop*, published in 2003. Currently she is working on a memoir focusing on her travel experiences illustrated with collages created while en route. She lives in Maryland with her husband, near their three children and five grandchildren.

NNELIZE GOEDBLOED was born on Celebes, Indonesia— a Dutch colony at the time—and spent her toddler years as a "guest" of the Emperor of Japan. After the war she and her parents (both physicians) were evacuated to Holland. Early exposure to creeping and crawling animal life inspired her to study parasitology and marine biology. While birthing her four children, she needed to be at home and thus started breeding pedigree Texel sheep and special chicken breeds. She served several years as a member of the board of pedigree sheep breeders of South Holland. Annelize started a company (BioClin) with her son, that now proudly holds a patent on a plant-derived polysaccharide with anti-infection properties. She has written clinical trials reports and lectures in English worldwide on scientific findings. The workshop in Ireland is her first effort in creative non-fiction writing. With thirteen grandchildren, the family breeding ventures are obviously continuing.

CONNIE GUTOWSKY was born in The Dalles, Oregon. She graduated from the University of Oregon and moved with her husband to his first teaching job in Tempe, Arizona, where she completed a Master's degree and their first son was born. They moved to Sacramento, California in 1968 where two other sons were born. Connie graduated from the University of the Pacific, McGeorge School of Law in 1975 and joined the Sacramento County Public Defender's Office, later going into private practice. She began studying and writing poetry when she retired in 2001. She loves her family, books, bridge, naps, friends, adventures, most people and mornings.

JENNY KARPMAN has written articles, essays, reviews and books on food, travel, human rights, and medicine. His pieces have appeared in *Best Travel Writing 2005*, Salon, *Troika, Journal of the American Medical Association, Circulation, Dallas Morning News, San Francisco Examiner, Newark Star Ledger, Pittsburgh Post Gazette, Pacific Sun, A.M. Costa Rica*, and many others. He was editor of *San Francisco Medicine and Chanticleer*. Dr. Karpman practiced medicine for more than thirty years as a cardiologist for Kaiser Permanente in San Francisco, served on the Marin County Human Rights Commission and on legislative committees of three California non-profits, and received the Benjamin Dreyfus Civil Liberties Lifetime Achievement Award from ACLU. Lenny and his wife Joan Hall live in Costa Rica on a farm, surrounded by a menagerie of rescued furry and feathered critters. They have three children and five grandchildren.

AURIE McANDISH KING is a travel writer whose essays have been published in anthologies such as *30 Days in Italy*, *The Thong Also Rises*, and the award-winning *The Kindness of Strangers*. Her work has also been published in the *San Francisco Chronicle Magazine* and aired on KUSF radio. Laurie earned her Master's degree in Internet-based education and publishes an online newsletter for travel writers at www.travelwritersnews.com. She is an officer and board member of Bay Area Travel Writers, and indulges her passions for travel and natural history as often as she possibly can. Laurie was the co-editor, with Linda Watanabe McFerrin, of *Hot Flashes: sexy little stories & poems*.

INDA WATANABE McFERRIN, poet, travel writer, novelist and teacher, is a contributor to numerous journals, newspapers, magazines, anthologies and online publications including the *San Francisco Examiner, The Washington Post, The San Francisco Chronicle Magazine, Modern Bride*, Travelers' Tales, Salon.com, and Women.com. She is the author of two poetry collections and the editor of the 4th edition of *Best Places Northern California*. A winner of the Nimrod International Journal Katherine Anne Porter Prize for Fiction, her work has also appeared in *Wild Places* and *American*

Fiction. Her novel, *Namako: Sea Cucumber* was published by Coffee House Press and named Best Book for the Teen-Age by the New York Public Library. Her collection of award-winning short stories, *The Hand of Buddha*, was published in 2000. She is also co-editor of a prize-winning travel anthology and the recently released *Hot Flashes: sexy little stories & poems.* Linda has served as a judge for the San Francisco Literary Awards and the Kiriyama Prize. She holds an undergraduate degree in Comparative Literature and a Master of Arts degree in Creative Writing and is the founder of Left Coast Writers (http://leftcoastwriters.com). When she is not on the road, she directs art, consults on communications and product development, and teaches Creative Writing. (www.lwmcferrin.com).

MARY JEAN PRAMIK, a coalminer's daughter and a great, great granddaughter of the Mongolian plain, has published copiously in medical journals, mined technical scientific metaphors, and launched three children. Mary Jean is the editor (a.k.a. ghost-writer) of the pharmaceutical thriller *Norethindrone; the First Three Decades*, available in most medical libraries, that relates the tortuous development of the first birth control pill. She has published in *Nature Biotechnology, Drug Topics,* and *Cosmetic Surgery News* as well as mainstream publications such as *Good Housekeeping* and the *National Enquirer*. Her poetry has appeared in college literary magazines and county fairs. She contributed to *Floating Through France: Life Between Locks on the Canal du Midi, Venturing in Southern Greece: The Vatika Odysseys* and *Odyssey* magazine. Mary Jean lives in the San Francisco Bay Area where she moonlights as a political activist and fledgling triathlete. She is currently at work on a novel entitled *GEM of Egypt* and a book of essays, *Know It All.*

About the Contributors

AIL STRICKLAND loves music, art, writing, languages. She has spent her life performing as a pianist in cabarets in San Francisco, symphonic orchestras and a little known eclectic country rock band called the Prairie Dogs. During forty-five years as a piano teacher who loves helping children discover music, Gail also pursued her passion for languages and foreign lands. She lived for months in Greece and Ireland and studied as an AFS Student in Stuttgart, Germany. In college she spent her time translating Homer and reading French philosophers. But beyond her love for all the arts, Gail has always sought the magic that lingers *between* the words, within the silent void we cannot paint or play or write. Only know. Gail has completed a novel set in ancient Greece, *Wild Garlic, Musky Wine,* and is working on a novel about the Dirty War in Argentina called *Monasteries for the Mad.*

HRYSA TSAKOPOULOS is a fourth year student at Georgetown University's School of Foreign Service in Washington D.C. studying International History. She is a native of Sacramento, California and loves to travel and teach English to underprivileged youth in the Sacramento and D.C. areas. During the early months of 2006 Chrysa co-wrote the script and acted in the independent film *Mosaics* which was released in early 2007. Her family is strongly involved in the promotion of Hellenism worldwide and has donated an exquisite collection of books to California State University, Sacramento, along with establishing chairs of Hellenic studies at major universities throughout the country. Her family has also contributed to the study of autism and founded the M.I.N.D. Institute at the University of California at Davis. Chrysa one day hopes to be involved in foreign policy and plans to continue to pursue her love for teaching youth. She is very proud to have been involved in the printing of *Venturing Through Southern Greece: The Vatika Odysseys.*

NN KATHLEEN URE lives in the San Francisco Bay Area. By day, she directs a non-profit organization affiliated with apparel company Levi Strauss & Co. By night she dreams about becoming the next Erma Bombeck. Throughout her varied career she has written advertising copy, product fliers, song lyrics, grants, business proposals and first-person essays. Her travel stories have been published in the anthologies *Floating through France: Life Between Locks on the Canal du Midi, Venturing through Southern Greece: The Vatika Odysseys*, and in the magazine *France Today*.

OREEN WOOD is a Canadian born writer who has either had a pen or keyboard in hand since she was a girl. As a medical rehabilitation professional she has a repertoire of academic papers, grant writing, non-fiction personal and memoir. Doreen has completed a book entitled, *Profoundly Ordinary*, stories of people who have survived a devastating disability. She also contributed to her husband's academic books. Whether it's writing stories about life with a disability, her own memoir, or personal essays, she writes with a keen eye to the emotional essence of a story, and maintains an incisive, yet fun-loving tone. She is also an avid traveler and her adventures give her food for thought and stories to weave. She is proud to be one of the authors in *Venturing in Southern Greece: The Vatika Odysseys*. Work on a memoir of her early years in Canada entitled *Sticks and Stones* is in progress. She has a grown son and daughter and lives in Larkspur, California.

Desmond O'Grady

ESMOND O'GRADY was born in Limerick, Ireland, in 1935 and spent most of his childhood in West Clare and the Irish-speaking districts of County Kerry. He left during the 1950s to teach and write in Paris, Rome and America. While a Teaching Fellow at Harvard University, he took his Masters and Doctorate in Celtic Languages and Literature. He has also taught at the American University in Cairo and at the University of Alexandria, Egypt.

From the late 1950s to the mid-1970s, while teaching in Rome, he was a founder member of the European Community of Writers, European editor of *The Transatlantic Review* and organized the Spoleto International Poetry Festival. He was an intimate friend and secretary to Ezra Pound for many years until the poet's death. Pound's influence is reflected in O'Grady's translations from a wide variety of poets in the classical and modern languages culminating in 1967 in *The Gododdin*, a free verse version of the Middle Welsh heroic poem of Aneirin.

Desmond O'Grady's publications number seventeen collections of poetry, including *The Road Taken: Poems 1956-1996* and *The Wandering Celt*; ten collections of translated poetry, among them *Trawling Tradition: Translation 1954-1994*, and *Selected Poems of C.P. Cavafy*; and prose memoirs of his literary acquaintances and friends such as Robert Lowell, A. Roland Holst, John Berryman, Pablo Neruda, and Samuel "Sam" Beckett. He is a member of Ireland's *Aosdána*, an association of people in Ireland who have achieved distinction in the arts. He now lives in Kinsale, County Cork, Ireland.

INDEX

250

Index

ABOUT THE EDITORS

BARBARA J. EUSER is a former political officer with the Foreign Service of the U.S. Department of State. As a director of the International Community Development Foundation, she has worked on projects in Bosnia, Somaliland, Zimbabwe, and Nepal. Her articles and essays have appeared in magazines and anthologies. She is the author of *Somaliland, Children of Dolpo* and *Take 'Em Along: Sharing the Wilderness with Your Children*, co-author of *A Climber's Climber: On the Trail with Carl Blaurock* and editor of *Bay Area Gardening* and *Gardening Among Friends*. In 2005, she organized the 2005 Writers Workshop on the Canal du Midi in France. She edited *Floating Through France: Life Between Locks on the Canal du Midi*, an anthology of essays by workshop participants. A founder of Writers Workshops International, she is co-editor of *Venturing in Southern Greece: The Vatika Odysseys*. She is married and has two grown daughters.

CONNIE BURKE left San Francisco, California in 1979. She set out for *Ithaka*, hoping to make her journey a long one, full of adventure, full of discovery. She has yet to return. On the way, she received a B.A. in English Literature, M.A. in the Humanities, and a Ph.D. in Education. She joined the English Faculty of the University of Maryland, European Division and The American College of Greece. Then she went on to establish and direct The Burke Institute for English Language Studies in Piraeus, Greece. Retired from academia, Connie resides in Piraeus where she served as the first President of Habitat for Humanity, Greater Athens. When she is not hammering nails and cleaning paintbrushes, she spends her time reading, writing, and celebrating life in the southern Peloponnesus. A founder of Writers Workshops International, she is co-editor of *Venturing in Southern Greece: The Vatika Odysseys*.